Procrastination

Discover How to Cure Laziness, Overcome Bad Habits, Develop Motivation, Improve Self-Discipline, Adopt a Success Mindset, and Increase Productivity, Even If You Are a Lazy Person

© Copyright 2020

All Rights Reserved. No part of this book may be reproduced in any form without permission in writing from the author. Reviewers may quote brief passages in reviews.

Disclaimer: No part of this publication may be reproduced or transmitted in any form or by any means, mechanical or electronic, including photocopying or recording, or by any information storage and retrieval system, or transmitted by email without permission in writing from the publisher.

While all attempts have been made to verify the information provided in this publication, neither the author nor the publisher assumes any responsibility for errors, omissions or contrary interpretations of the subject matter herein.

This book is for entertainment purposes only. The views expressed are those of the author alone, and should not be taken as expert instruction or commands. The reader is responsible for his or her own actions.

Adherence to all applicable laws and regulations, including international, federal, state and local laws governing professional licensing, business practices, advertising and all other aspects of doing business in the US, Canada, UK or any other jurisdiction is the sole responsibility of the purchaser or reader.

Neither the author nor the publisher assumes any responsibility or liability whatsoever on the behalf of the purchaser or reader of these materials. Any perceived slight of any individual or organization is purely unintentional.

Contents

INTRODUCTION 1
CHAPTER 1: WHY PROCRASTINATION HAPPENS 2
    THE NEED FOR PERFECTION 3
    FEAR OF THE UNKNOWN 4
    DELAYING FOR A BETTER TIME 4
    CHOOSING EASIER TASKS FIRST 5
    LOW ENERGY LEVELS 6
    LACK OF DIRECTION 7
    CONSTANT DISTRACTIONS 8
    FEAR OF COMMITMENT 9
CHAPTER 2: THE PSYCHOLOGY OF PROCRASTINATION 10
    SITUATIONAL VS. CHRONIC 10
    AROUSAL PROCRASTINATION 12
    AVOIDER PROCRASTINATION 13
    DECISIONAL PROCRASTINATION 15
    THE ROLE OF GUILT IN PROCRASTINATING 16
CHAPTER 3: PROCRASTINATION VS. LAZINESS 18

PERSONALITY VS. BEHAVIOR 19
THE TRUE NATURE OF LAZINESS 20
THE TRUE NATURE OF PROCRASTINATION 23

CHAPTER 4: STEPS TO CURING PROCRASTINATION 26

UNDERSTAND YOUR REASONS FOR PROCRASTINATING 27
IDENTIFY ANY NEGATIVE THOUGHTS AND CHANGE THEM 28
CONFRONT LAZINESS 29
ORGANIZE YOUR LIFE 30
BREAK DOWN LARGE PROJECTS INTO SMALLER TASKS 31
CREATE GOOD HABITS 32

CHAPTER 5: TWEAKING YOUR THOUGHTS TO AVOID PROCRASTINATION 34

THE CHEMISTRY OF SUCCESS/FAILURE 35
CHANGE YOUR PERSPECTIVE 36
CHANGE THE VERNACULAR 39
NEGATIVITY AS A POSITIVE 40

CHAPTER 6: TEN PROVEN WAYS TO BEAT LAZINESS 43

BE FORGIVING 43
TAKE THE FIRST STEP 44
BEGIN EARLY 45
TAKE PLENTY OF BREAKS 45
ELIMINATE DISTRACTIONS 46
KEEP YOUR MOTIVATION REFRESHED 47
DECLUTTER YOUR LIFE 48
ACCEPT SETBACKS 48
SURROUND YOURSELF WITH POSITIVE ENERGY 49
EMBRACE LAZINESS 50

CHAPTER 7: PLAN IT OUT: SIX STEPS TO GETTING THINGS DONE ... 51

SET SMART GOALS 52
CREATE THE RIGHT ENVIRONMENT 53
SET SOME EASY RULES 54
MAINTAIN YOUR ENERGY LEVELS 55

Set Yourself Up for Success 56
Find What Works for You 57

CHAPTER 8: HOW TO GET STARTED ON ANY PROJECT NOW 59
Get Excited 59
Write it Down 61
Commit Time to Your Project 62
Commit Resources to Your Project 63
Create Incentives 65

CHAPTER 9: BAD HABITS THAT STIFLE YOUR PRODUCTIVITY (PLUS PRODUCTIVITY HACKS) 67
Multitasking 68
Constantly Focusing on the Big Picture 69
Being Unstructured 70
Striving for Perfection 71
Being Overbooked 72
Waiting for Better Conditions 73

CHAPTER 10: THE SUCCESS MINDSET: FIVE TIPS FROM SUCCESS EXPERTS 75
Define Success 76
Create a Growth Mindset 77
Become Self-Aware 78
Ignore the Opinions of Others 80
Become the Change You Desire 82

CHAPTER 11: DAILY HABITS FOR MOTIVATION AND SELF-DISCIPLINE 85
Wake Up at a Decent Hour 86
Perform a Small Task First Thing in the Morning 87
Visualize Your Dream 87
Visualize Your Day 88
Write Down a Task List 89
Cross off Each Item as You Accomplish It 90
Take Time to Reflect at the End of the Day 90

GO TO BED AT A DECENT HOUR 91
CHAPTER 12: RELAPSE IS NOT THE END OF THE WORLD 93
    EMBRACE THE SETBACKS 94
    LEARN TO CELEBRATE THE POSITIVES 95
    SEEK OUT FRESH MOTIVATION 96
CONCLUSION 98
SOURCES 99

Introduction

Countless books have been written on the subject of procrastination, offering numerous tips and tricks on how to overcome it and create a more successful, productive life. Unfortunately, most of these books fall short of their goal for one reason or another, leaving the reader with little to show for their efforts. Fortunately, this book addresses procrastination in a new and comprehensive way, offering insight into the causes of procrastination in order to provide a deeper understanding of the subject. Furthermore, a clinical evaluation of the psychology behind procrastination will enable you to recognize mindsets and personality traits that impact your productivity from the deepest levels. Subsequently, this book will help you to not just change your habits and behaviors; it will enable you to achieve true personal transformation, the kind that will enable you to pursue and achieve all of your goals, ambitions, and dreams. Finally, the methods and techniques provided will help you to create a clear plan for eliminating procrastination from your life once and for all. By the time you finish reading this book, you will have all the information and tools needed to not only eliminate procrastination, but to live the life you have always desired, one full of purpose, success, and true happiness.

Chapter 1: Why Procrastination Happens

While this book may be the first attempt to solve procrastination for some readers, for many, it will be one of several books they have read on the subject. The question is, why do most books fail to provide significant and effective tools for overcoming procrastination? The most common reason is that they treat procrastination as a singular problem, providing a "one size fits all" perspective that fails to address the numerous causes of procrastination. Since procrastination has many different causes, it stands to reason that it will also have many different cures. Therefore, before you start searching for the methods and tools needed to overcome procrastination once and for all, you must first determine the precise issues that lead to your procrastination in the first place. Believe it or not, there are eight unique behaviors and mindsets that serve to create different forms of procrastination. This chapter will explore each of those mindsets and behaviors, helping you to identify the ones that are keeping you from achieving your goals. As this chapter is focused on the causes of procrastination, it won't discuss the solutions, leaving those for the following chapters where they can be discussed in greater depth.

The Need for Perfection

For many, getting a task or project done simply isn't enough. Instead, they must also achieve perfection. The finished product needs to be the best, or else it's not worth doing. While this perspective may seem to be the stuff of success, the truth of the matter is that the need for perfection is one of the chief causes of procrastination. The more a person requires perfection, the less likely they are to start a project or task for fear that the end result might fall short. Needless to say, this is a significant obstacle to overcome, especially in a world where anything less than perfection is seen as inferior.

The problem with perfection is that it is a virtual impossibility. Almost nothing in life is perfect, which stands to reason. After all, if everything was perfect, then perfection itself would be seen as ordinary, thereby losing its significance. The very fact that perfection is still held as an ideal, underscores its rarity. However, sometimes the problem isn't even with perfection; rather, it is the fear of not being as good as someone else. When you compare your results to the results of others, it can have the effect of making you feel inferior, and that can significantly reduce your desire to start a project seeing as you lack the confidence to achieve a result others will admire.

Perhaps the biggest problem with the need for perfection is the vicious cycle it creates. The fear of falling short will cause you to put off starting a task, which in turn reduces the amount of time you have to complete that task. As the time available shrinks, the chance of achieving success also shrinks, causing you to lose even more confidence, thus procrastinating further still. In the end, the fear of imperfection is often a self-fulfilling prophecy, one that could be largely avoided simply by starting a task or project when you have the most time available to get it done.

Fear of the Unknown

The next cause of procrastination, which affects millions of people, is the fear of the unknown. This fear can present itself in many ways, but more often than not, it takes the form of a fear of disaster. A good example of this is if you ever put off trying a new restaurant because you weren't sure how good their food would be, or whether or not you would have a good time. Although this isn't procrastination as such, it is the same fear of a negative outcome that causes many people to put off actions for as long as possible.

A good example of procrastination due to the fear of the unknown is when a person puts off going to the doctor to get a particular pain or symptom checked out. Many people only go to the doctor when that particular symptom becomes so bad that it impacts their day-to-day lives in a significantly negative way. More often than not, the reason they put off seeing their doctor is the fear of what the doctor might say. Worst case scenarios, including surgery, a terminal diagnosis, or some other extreme result, can flood a person's heart and mind, causing them to put off the appointment until it becomes absolutely necessary.

Needless to say, the results of procrastinating in this way can prove extremely detrimental, especially in the case of a health issue. Modern medicine can cure or at least treat most illnesses when caught in time. Thus, when you procrastinate, you only decrease your chances of getting cured, making this another example of a self-fulfilling prophecy, one that could have been avoided if you had taken prompt action instead of putting things off until the last possible minute.

Delaying for a Better Time

A less sinister cause of procrastination is that of delaying for a better time. How many times have you decided to put off a task or project until later, convincing yourself that you would somehow have more time, energy, or resources at that later moment? Needless to say, there are times when you won't have the right amount of time, energy, or resources to get things done, but this isn't really about that. This is more a matter of waiting for the "right time." And, as most people come to realize at one point or another in their lives, the right time rarely ever comes.

One reason why the right time never comes is that a person's habits rarely change. Thus, if you have low energy on your day off that causes you to put off a task for another day, unless your low energy is the result of a bad night's sleep, sickness, or some other out-of-the-ordinary circumstance, there is no reason to expect your energy levels will be any better the next time around. This leaves you in the very same boat on your next day off, lacking the energy needed to inspire you to address the task or project at hand.

Not having the right amount of money or other resources can also cause a person to put off a project indefinitely, waiting for that golden moment when their life will change, and suddenly they will have more money than usual for no apparent reason. It is one thing if you conscientiously choose to put a project off in order to build up the cash or resources needed to accomplish it. That is simply good planning. What makes it procrastination is when you just expect circumstances to improve without any effort on your part. The simple truth is that the time and resources at your disposal now are probably the same as they will be at any other time, so this is as good a moment to start the task as any.

Choosing Easier Tasks First

Sometimes procrastination can show up in more subtle ways. This is especially true when you have numerous tasks to complete within a given time frame. Ordinarily, procrastination is easy to spot, as it is when you put off the single task or project on your plate for another time. However, in the event that you have more than one project, you can actually procrastinate while still appearing to be productive. This is when you put off the bigger or more daunting project until later, choosing to accomplish the easier, more enjoyable tasks first. Again, even though you are still productive, the act of putting off that larger task is, in fact, a significant form of procrastination.

The problem with this type of procrastination is that it can prove to get worse as time progresses, becoming the proverbial snowball gaining mass as it rolls downhill. More often than not, a person chooses the easier tasks first because they are more fun. Choosing to put off boring or tedious tasks until later won't make them any better. Instead, because you've spent your day doing the fun things first, the task you put off will only seem even more tedious or undesirable later on. This is especially true if the task requires a great deal of energy, since your energy levels will be even more depleted by the time you address the task at the last possible moment.

Another reason why this form of procrastination is perhaps the most dangerous is that you can convince yourself that you aren't actually procrastinating at all. Because you are doing other activities, you feel productive, and therefore you lack the guilt that sheer laziness can create. Unfortunately, more often than not, this "productivity" is merely an illusion. Although the smaller, more enjoyable tasks need to be done, they don't provide the same amount of results as the larger, more tedious projects. Therefore, despite appearing to be productive, the fact is that you are actually wasting as much time as if you weren't doing anything at all.

Low Energy Levels

Any task or project, regardless of how large or small, will require a certain amount of energy to get done. Whether that energy is physical or mental, it can often be tempting to put off a task if you don't feel as though your current energy levels are high enough for what needs to be accomplished.

The bottom line is that your energy levels usually start high and diminish as the day progresses, not the other way around. Therefore, if you feel as though you don't have the energy for something first thing in the morning, you definitely won't have it later in the afternoon. Instead, the longer you put off a task or project for, the lower your energy levels will be by the time you get around to working on that project. This means that you will feel even worse about accomplishing your task, when you are left with no other choice, and you can't put it off any longer.

Stress can play a significant role in this scenario, as well. If you are unmotivated due to the stress of the project or task at hand, putting it off until later will only make matters worse. Now, in addition to being a stressful task, you have the added anxiety of having far less time in which to complete it. Although it can seem like you are doing yourself a favor by putting off the big, unpleasant tasks until later, the longer you delay, the worse things get.

Lack of Direction

So far, the reasons for procrastination have focused on poor decision making, a lack of discipline, and other behaviors that are largely associated with laziness or a lack of motivation. There are, however, some causes that affect even those with rock-solid willpower and unshakable resolve. One such cause is a lack of direction, which is when you don't know exactly where to start on a project, or what direction to take with a specific task. Even when you have all the energy and discipline in the world, if you don't know how to tackle the task at hand, it can make it seem like getting started is all but impossible.

A good way to imagine this is if you are sitting in your car with nowhere to go. You can have all the time in the world and a full tank of gas, but if you don't know where you are supposed to drive next, then there is no reason for you to leave where you are. This is what happens when people don't get thorough, precise directions on how to perform a task or project. Without proper direction, any effort could be wasted, or even worse, prove counterproductive in the long run.

Therefore, procrastinating is seen as a safe bet, ensuring no mistakes are made and no effort wasted.

The problem here is that "kicking the can down the road," so to speak, doesn't solve the problem. Sure, taking uncertain action isn't the best plan either, but doing nothing will only ensure that the situation fails to improve. Putting off action while trying to find direction is one thing, but simply putting off action isn't going to get the job done. Therefore, this is one of those areas where recognizing the cause of procrastination can make all the difference. Once you get the direction you need, the procrastination will be instantly solved, allowing you to accomplish the task at hand without further delay.

Constant Distractions

Perhaps the most common cause of procrastination is the constant barrage of distractions that affect everyone at all times. Everything from cell phones to radios, TVs, and other sources of noise and entertainment can tempt even the strongest willed person away from the task they are performing, causing them to delay their efforts "just for a little while." Unfortunately, the sheer number of distractions available can make "just a little while" turn into hours or even days in extreme cases. The bottom line is that everyone's mind wants to have fun and is therefore easily tempted away from any work when a more enjoyable alternative presents itself.

However, not all distractions have to be pleasant in nature. The truth of the matter is that there are just as many work-related distractions as there are distractions of any other kind. Constant phone calls, people interrupting to ask questions, and even more work being added to your inbox, can distract your attention and effort more than your cell phone ever could. The problem in these cases is that since they are work-related, such distractions are seen as acceptable, making procrastination almost justified. Needless to say, no matter what form procrastination takes, the end result is always the same—

putting off accomplishing the task at hand, thereby reducing efficiency, overall productivity, and the quality of the results.

Fear of Commitment

The eighth and final cause of procrastination to consider is the fear of commitment. This is when you know how much time and energy a particular project will take, making it overwhelming in scope. Fear of commitment is probably the main reason why just about everyone has that big project that they just never get around to. Whether it's painting your house, cleaning out your basement, or replacing your old, worn-out deck, any project that will require large amounts of cash, time, and effort, is one that can easily be pushed back to another time.

This is another case where procrastination isn't necessarily the result of bad habits or a negative mindset. Instead, the sheer scope of some projects can make them overwhelming for anyone, even the most inspired and energetic of people. The real problem here is that when such a large project is treated as a single entity, it can seem insurmountable. As a result, such projects get put off for one reason or another, until they either become an absolute necessity or they just get canceled altogether.

Chapter 2: The Psychology of Procrastination

Most books and videos that try to address the root causes of procrastination tend to approach things in terms of behavior and habits. Poor time management, a lack of discipline, an inability to avoid distractions and the like, are usually cited as the critical issues when it comes to the causes of procrastination in its various forms. However, recent studies have shown that there is another dimension to procrastination, one that affects people on a deeper level. That dimension is the psychology of procrastination. This approach argues that elements such as self-esteem, guilt, thrill-seeking behavior, and fear of failure contribute not only to procrastination but also to the other behaviors and habits that are usually seen as the cause. This chapter will explore the psychology of procrastination, showing how many of the behaviors that are commonly seen as causes are, in fact, the symptoms of a greater issue.

Situational vs. Chronic

In order to effectively address the issue of procrastination, the first thing you need to ask yourself is what kind of procrastinator you are. The simple truth of the matter is that just about everyone procrastinates at one time or another, meaning that procrastination itself isn't a rare or dangerous behavior as such. However, studies done by psychology professor Joseph Ferrari at DePaul University, have determined that as many as twenty percent of people are what can be considered "chronic procrastinators." These are the people who procrastinate on a regular basis, regardless of the task or project at hand. In contrast, the remaining eighty percent of people simply put things off from time to time, usually for reasons that are easy to understand, such as low motivation, feeling overwhelmed, or a lack of time and resources. Therefore, before you start trying to change your behaviors, the first thing you need to do is determine how serious your procrastination really is.

If you are a situational procrastinator, then you will feel pretty confident when it comes to getting things done on time on a regular basis. Furthermore, you probably won't have any issues with getting started on a project or task, as you will have the confidence and motivation needed to get things rolling without delay. When it comes to the large, undesirable projects such as painting your house or going to the doctor, you might struggle with maintaining your usual discipline and starting in a responsible and timely manner. In this case, the basic methods for overcoming procrastination will be enough to change your behavior on those rare occasions, helping you to raise your game and be more consistent in your ability to tackle any task or project with confidence and determination.

Alternatively, if you are a chronic procrastinator, then you know that the rare occurrence is when you address a task or project in a timely and responsible manner, not when you put it off for another time. For one reason or another, you struggle to find the motivation to start things off on the right foot. Day after day sees you put things off to the last minute, thereby increasing your stress, decreasing your performance, and even undermining your chances of success. Eventually, your reputation suffers, and you are left living a life far beneath your true potential. If this describes the situation you find yourself in, then you are a chronic procrastinator. Numerous studies around the world have concluded that this chronic condition is the result of psychological issues that need to be addressed at the root. Fortunately, these studies have also broken down the various psychological explanations into a few groups that are easy to recognize, and thus easy to manage and even overcome.

Arousal Procrastination

The first type of procrastination to consider is that of arousal procrastination. This is the form of procrastination most commonly associated with extreme thrill-seekers. Ordinary thrill-seekers might choose to go skydiving for fun, enjoying the rush as they freefall from a plane before deploying their parachute and safely returning to the ground. In contrast, extreme thrill seekers will not only go skydiving; they will wait until the very last second before deploying their parachute, putting their lives at even greater risk in the process. The need for that extra adrenaline rush makes them take already considerable challenges and add another layer of danger to them. Such people may not even be aware of their need for this adrenaline rush, resulting in them being a victim to their addiction and the behaviors associated with it.

In terms of procrastination, arousal procrastinators will put off big, important tasks or projects until the last minute in order to feel that exhilaration of staring disaster in the face. Ordinary people would get started on such projects as early as possible, thus ensuring a safe timeframe within which to get the project done. This is like the ordinary person deploying their parachute as soon as possible in order to ensure their safety while skydiving. However, the same rush that comes from deploying the parachute at the last minute is the rush that comes from delivering a mere project seconds before the deadline expires. This gives them the experience of escaping destruction each and every day without having to go to the lengths of going skydiving or performing some other death-defying activity.

What makes this form of procrastination unique is that it isn't the result of self-destructive behavior or low self-esteem. Nor is it the byproduct of laziness or a poor work ethic. Instead, it is the result of an addiction to the adrenaline that accompanies high levels of anxiety, usually associated with life and death scenarios. This is why many methods of overcoming procrastination fall short of producing results for arousal procrastinators, as they don't address the true cause of their behavior.

Avoider Procrastination

The second form of procrastination to consider is that of avoider procrastination. This is perhaps the most common of all forms, and it is what keeps most people from achieving their full potential. Simply put, someone in this category will avoid performing a task or project for as long as possible because they are afraid of the outcome. More often than not, this is reduced to a basic fear of failure. While the fear of failure does play a large role in avoider procrastination, it is not the only form of fear that is present. In fact, many studies have shown that the fear of success also contributes to avoider procrastination. Therefore, if you find that you avoid doing things until the last minute for fear of one type or another, then this is the form of procrastination that impacts you.

Needless to say, failure is something that most people want to avoid at all costs. As a result, if you feel as though you aren't up to the task at hand, a fear of failure will cause you to put off that task for as long as possible, thereby avoiding the issue and the failure it threatens to bring. This usually stems from low self-esteem, meaning that you feel inadequate for the task you have been given. The stronger your fear of failure, the longer you will avoid performing the task at hand. In this case, however, most people do bring themselves to tackle the project, usually successfully, just in the nick of time.

Another form of avoider procrastination addresses the fear of failure in a more self-destructive way. This is when instead of overcoming the fear of failure and accomplishing the task, you actually sabotage your efforts, failing to complete the task or project in the time given. More often than not, this is an attempt to shift the blame from your perceived inadequacies to the lack of time available as a result of your procrastination. What makes this form worse is that the fear of failure is so absolute that the individual simply refuses to take any chance at all. Rather than trying to accomplish the task or project, they actually create a situation where failure is guaranteed. Known as "self-handicapping," this is a behavior that results from the lowest levels of self-esteem and self-confidence.

Finally, there is the fear of success, something that most people don't even realize exists. There are two main reasons for fearing success. First, there is the fear that by succeeding, you will invite greater expectations on your performance. In other words, when you go above and beyond, delivering results against all the odds, you will be expected to maintain that level of effort on a regular basis. This stands to reason as most companies come to expect the best from their employees. Therefore, once you demonstrate your best, you open the floodgates for your boss to expect that level of performance each and every time. This will only increase your workload, and thus your day-to-day stress. Subsequently, you avoid putting your best foot forward since the consequences of success are seemingly negative in nature.

The second reason why a person fears success is that they don't want to make others look bad. This usually takes place in competitive environments where kind-hearted people can't stand the thought of being the reason others lose out. Rather than achieving success at the expense of others, such a person will avoid a task or project, reducing their chances of success as a result. It's a bit like faking an injury to allow someone else to win the race. This type of procrastination is pretty rare, but it is no less detrimental than any of the other forms. The overall result is a reduction of effort, thereby keeping you from achieving the success you are actually capable of.

Decisional Procrastination

Decisional procrastination affects both situational and chronic procrastinators alike. In short, it is when you avoid a task or project because you either don't know enough to make the right decision to get started, or you simply can't handle the responsibility of making decisions because you are afraid of making a mistake. In the end, the fear of making bad decisions that lead to failure will cause a person to commit decisional procrastination for as long as possible.

In the situational case, this is usually the result of being unclear about the task at hand. A lack of instruction, training, or general direction can undermine a person's confidence when it comes to knowing where to start. This doesn't necessarily mean that the individual is suffering from low self-esteem; rather, it means that they find themselves in a situation where uncertainty creates the fear of getting things wrong. By procrastinating, they can avoid making those decisions, thereby burying their head in the sand for a while, hoping the situation will resolve itself by some magic or miracle. Unfortunately, such magic and miracles are usually not forthcoming, meaning that the individual is left to face their demons later on, whether they like it or not.

In the case of a chronic procrastinator, decisional procrastination comes from a lack of confidence when making decisions. Thus, instead of this being a one-off situation, it is one that occurs on a regular basis. Most people in this category simply can't handle the stress of being responsible for the outcome of any decision they have to make. Therefore, they avoid making decisions as often and for as long as possible. Although many bring themselves to make those painful decisions at the last moment, some will procrastinate long enough to ensure failure rather than take the chance of causing the failure with the decisions they would have had to make. This allows them to blame their failure on a lack of time, thereby absolving them of any personal blame.

The Role of Guilt in Procrastinating

The final thing to consider is the role that guilt plays when it comes to procrastination. Regardless of the type of procrastination a person practices, one thing that just about all procrastinators share is the feeling of guilt. More often than not, this guilt is seen as a consequence of procrastination. However, recent studies have discovered a startling new angle, one that suggests that rather than being the consequence of procrastination, guilt can actually be the cause. This means that it's the guilt that leads to self-destructive behavior, not the other way around.

Doctor David Maloney is a psychotherapist who has explored the many causes of procrastination. In addition to the common psychological causes, namely low self-esteem or the fear of failure, he has discovered that guilt can cause a person to procrastinate, even to the point of failing to finish a task or project altogether. His conclusion is that this behavior is a form of self-punishment, the sabotaging of success due to guilt or some other emotional trauma that can be traced to the individual's past. Only by recognizing the source of that guilt or trauma can a person effectively end the self-destructive behavior and begin to achieve the success they both desire and deserve.

In order to identify most causes of procrastination, you need to ask yourself why you are avoiding the task at hand. However, in this case, the question you would ask is why you feel undeserving of the success within your reach. After all, that is the overall reason for this type of procrastination—the deliberate self-sabotaging in order to prevent yourself from achieving success. Only by searching your history, including all emotional traumas and other events that could explain your feeling of guilt, can you find the reason you feel unworthy of living a life of success and happiness. Once you have that piece of the puzzle, all procrastination habits and behaviors will disappear as your subconscious mind won't need them any longer. After all, once the guilt has resolved, the need for punishment will no longer exist.

Reasons for this type of self-sabotage can come in all different forms. For example, if you cheated in order to win in the past, you might feel guilty of the success you achieved, thereby causing you to surrender current and future successes in order to atone for your wrongdoing. This sense of atonement can also be the result of hurting others in the past due to being overly competitive, or the guilt of seeing someone suffer as the result of your success, even if you didn't do anything wrong. All in all, this type of guilt usually has the effect of taking the joy out of success, thereby causing a person to avoid success at all costs.

Another reason behind guilt-driven procrastination is the need to make things harder on yourself, which can stem from a feeling of always having an advantage over others, such as being favored or having more resources at your disposal. In order to assuage your guilt for having such an advantage, you procrastinate, thereby undermining your chances of success. This creates a more level playing field in your mind, thus making the game fairer. In the end, the sense of guilt can always be traced to an issue of self-esteem, one that you feel can only be corrected by punishment. Subsequently, the only cure for guilt-driven procrastination is to forgive yourself for any past mistakes or any sense of entitlement, so that you can get on with achieving the success you are capable of.

Chapter 3: Procrastination vs. Laziness

One of the biggest problems when it comes to overcoming procrastination is that most books address procrastination as a symptom of laziness. The common belief is that anyone who is properly motivated will naturally tackle any task or project without delay, thereby avoiding any type of procrastination. Alternatively, when someone puts off tasks or projects, it suggests that they lack initiative, energy, or ambition. At best, they lack the desire to grow and succeed; at worst, they are downright lazy. Surprisingly enough, the link between laziness and procrastination is often unwarranted. In fact, one is a matter of personality, whereas the other is a matter of behavior. Ignoring this fundamental truth can result in misdiagnosing an individual as being lazy simply for putting off the task or project at hand. Therefore, in order to properly recognize the root cause of procrastination, it is vital to first understand the difference between laziness and procrastination. Only then can you begin to take the proper steps to overcome procrastination within your life once and for all.

Personality vs. Behavior

As already mentioned, the biggest difference between procrastination and laziness is that one is a matter of personality, whereas the other is a matter of behavior. This is a distinction that most people fail to understand, causing them to assume the two conditions are one and the same, when, in fact, nothing could be further from the truth. The best way to understand the difference between personality and behavior is to see personality as who a person is and behavior as what a person does. Although at first glance, these concepts might appear to be virtually identical, upon closer inspection, their differences become abundantly clear.

Who you are as a person can have a number of influences. First and foremost are your genetics. Long-term studies—like the Minnesota Twin Family Study undertaken by the University of Minnesota—have revealed that personality traits can be passed from generation to generation, even becoming stronger with each generation. A good way to portray this would be in terms of physical strength. Although a person can develop physical strength by going to the gym and working out, they can also inherit a certain "natural strength," one that is the consequence of having a family history of strong men and women in their family tree. Thus, a person may grow up to have a certain level of strength simply because of the nature of their genetic makeup.

Additionally, strength can be the result of environmental conditions such as upbringing. Children who have to perform physical labor from an early age will grow up to be physically stronger than those who grow up in less physically demanding circumstances. The strength such a child possesses later in life will be of a more natural sort, one that they don't have to maintain through exercise as such. This makes their strength a part of who they are, rather than the consequence of what they do.

In contrast, a behavior is when a person chooses to perform an action in order to achieve a particular result. When a person chooses to go to the gym and work out, they are performing the behavior that will make them strong. In time they may be as strong if not stronger than the person who is strong due to genetics or upbringing. However, they will have to work at developing and maintaining that strength. Once they stop exercising and working out, their body will return to its natural state, thereby losing the strength they have developed by going to the gym.

This is how personality and behavior works. Personality is who a person is inherent. Since procrastination is behavior by definition, no one is a natural procrastinator. They might be a poor decision-maker or have low self-esteem, but the procrastination itself will be a symptom of those traits, not the trait itself. Laziness, in contrast, is a personality trait, one that can be passed down through genetics, or developed by environmental factors such as upbringing. As such, laziness isn't the action itself; rather, it is the personality trait behind the action. This is why highly motivated people can procrastinate, and why a typically lazy person may jump in and work on a task without delay. Fortunately, once you determine whether you suffer from a matter of personality or behavior, laziness or procrastination, you can take the necessary steps to change your direction and begin achieving the success you both desire and deserve.

The True Nature of Laziness

If you look up the word "laziness" in the dictionary, you will find that it refers to a general disinclination to perform any kind of work or chore that would require significant effort. The Latin root for laziness is "indolentia," which describes a mindset that lacks trouble or pain. This underscores the previous point that laziness is a personality trait as opposed to behavior. Putting off work or avoiding work is the behavior, but the desire to do so is the mindset, and that is what makes all the difference.

A 2012 study by researchers at Vanderbilt University, which was published in the *Journal of Neuroscience*, showed that lazy people actually have a different neurological makeup to the average person. Everyone is driven by a chemical reaction to stimuli, resulting in making something desirable or undesirable. Exercise is a good example of this phenomenon. Almost everyone experiences a release of dopamine when eating certain foods or participating in sexual activity. Dopamine is a chemical produced in the body that causes a feeling of pleasure. However, while most people also get that release of dopamine during and after exercising, "lazy" people do not. This means that rather than having a positive mental and emotional impact, exercise takes on an undesirable nature. The result is that people who are lazy simply avoid exercise as it fails to provide any pleasurable incentive.

Although this may seem strange, it isn't very hard to understand when you consider just how pleasure-driven the average person really is. You can see this in the foods that people eat. The main reason why so many people are overweight is that they eat foods heavy in fat, sugar, or salt. This is because those foods taste good, meaning they get pleasure from eating them. Just as eating raw broccoli doesn't provide that same feeling of pleasure and bliss to the average eater, so too, does work and exercise fail to provide a sense of contentment or pleasure for a lazy person. As a result, people who are lazy avoid work the same way as the average person avoids eating a salad for lunch.

This is where the main difference between procrastination and laziness comes into play. Whereas a procrastinator has good intentions at first, a lazy person lacks any intention of getting things done. Thus, rather than putting something off for another time, or avoiding a task until the last possible minute, a lazy person won't sign on for that task in the first place. Instead, they will avoid any work altogether, always finding shortcuts and loopholes that allow them to put in the least amount of effort necessary. In fact, lazy people often spend more effort trying to avoid a task than the task would have actually required in the first place. However, since the task promises pain and unhappiness, any amount of effort is worthwhile if it helps them to avoid having to do the task.

Another way to imagine this is to give yourself the choice of going to the beach or going to the dentist. No one in their right mind would ever choose to go to the dentist over the beach. Going to the beach is a win for anyone. This is exactly how a lazy person's mindset works. Anything and everything that resembles work is a trip to the dentist for them. No good ever comes of it, only pain and misery. Therefore, they conscientiously choose to do no work since that way they can avoid the pain and misery. No effort is too great if it spares them a trip to the proverbial dentist. Thus, they will put themselves in a position where they can consistently avoid work, putting in as little effort as possible just to get by.

Fortunately, even though laziness is a personality trait, one that has been shown to be genetic, as well as the result of environmental conditions, it is something that can be overcome. Just as the risk for any hereditary physical illness that runs in the family can be reduced by taking appropriate action, so too, can appropriate actions be taken to develop better habits that overcome the tendency of laziness. The key is to recognize the fact that your behavior is the result of laziness so that you can be sure the actions you take are effective. The best way to be sure is to ask yourself the following questions:

- Do you avoid any and all kinds of work?
- Does work make you feel exhausted?
- Do you lack a sense of satisfaction when you finish a task or project?
- Do you feel less energized after exercising?
- Are you likely to avoid even the simplest of tasks for no reason?

If you answered "yes" to most or all of these questions, then you aren't struggling with procrastination, rather you are struggling with laziness. Fortunately, this book will provide proven methods for overcoming laziness and creating habits that will enable you to live a more productive, successful life, one that brings you the happiness you deserve.

The True Nature of Procrastination

Unlike laziness, procrastination is not the act of avoiding any type of work or labor altogether. Instead, procrastination has a very different meaning, one that involves time as opposed to effort. The Latin root of the word literally means to put off until tomorrow. This fits the general understanding of the term, namely the act of pushing a task or project as far back as possible. Although some forms of procrastination can result in failing to complete a task or project, most simply result in the task or project not being completed until the last possible minute. This makes a huge difference in terms of the mindset and personality of someone who procrastinates compared to someone who is inherently lazy. And this is why procrastination and laziness need to be treated as very different conditions.

One of the first things to note is that procrastination is a behavior, not a personality trait or a mindset. It is an action, not a state of being. As such, it can be caused by such things as poor habits, a lack of direction, or any number of issues that can easily be resolved. Someone who procrastinates, therefore, isn't necessarily "broken" or in need of a major overhaul. Instead, they just need to break some bad habits and replace them with better, more productive habits. This makes the process a lot easier, as the mindset of a procrastinator is usually positive in nature, meaning that better habits will take hold quickly and start producing results right away.

However, the first step is to determine whether or not you are a procrastinator, as opposed to being lazy. As mentioned before, people who are lazy lack the intention of doing any work at all. In contrast, a procrastinator tends to have the best intentions. They take on a list of projects or tasks with the expectation of completing them, thereby achieving success and satisfaction as a result. This goes back to the studies conducted that determined the role dopamine plays in a person's work ethic. Usually people tend to feel satisfaction and pleasure from accomplishing goals. Even if they have to put in vast amounts of effort and time to accomplish a task, they will feel as though it was worth it in the end. In fact, the harder the task, the greater the sense of accomplishment the individual experiences when it is finally completed. Therefore, rather than avoiding work completely, a procrastinator will eagerly accept a task at first, only to put off working on it later on.

When a procrastinator puts off a task or project, they usually fill their time with less important tasks and projects, thereby still maintaining some level of productivity. Alternatively, laziness leads people to avoid a task or project and spend their time being idle and unproductive, thereby producing no results at all. This is perhaps the best proof that a person who procrastinates isn't actually lazy, rather they are uninspired or overwhelmed, resulting in them losing confidence in a task rather than lacking the desire to see it completed.

A good way to see this difference is to revisit the example of going to the dentist or going to the beach. The lazy person will choose to go to the beach every single time, without ever giving the dentist a second thought. Alternatively, the procrastinator might actually choose the dentist on occasion, even if they put it off for as long as possible due to their fear of the experience. Or, they might experience a feeling of guilt each time they choose the beach, eventually causing them to choose the dentist as they know that is the right choice to make. This is how they view work. Although part of them is drawn to the easier path, they have a sense of responsibility that prevents them from shirking work altogether. No matter how undesirable the task or project proves to be, a procrastinator will almost always get to it in the end, as they know it is the right thing to do. Fortunately, this inherent sense of value means that procrastinators aren't afraid of work or effort; they are simply afraid of getting started on a particular task or project in a timely way. Thus, a simple tweaking of habits and perspectives is all it takes to overcome procrastination.

In order to determine whether or not you struggle with procrastination, as opposed to laziness, simply ask yourself the following questions:

- Do you generally enjoy being productive?
- Does work give you a sense of purpose?
- Do you feel a sense of satisfaction when you finish a project?
- Do you usually feel energized and refreshed after exercising?
- Do you usually accomplish all your tasks on a regular basis?

If you answered "yes" to most or all of these questions, then you are not lazy. Instead, you are a regular individual who struggles to face those large and unpleasant projects in a timely manner. Fortunately, the solution to this situation is fairly easy and straightforward, meaning that you can fix your behaviors and begin enjoying a more productive and satisfying life as a result.

Chapter 4: Steps to Curing Procrastination

The process of curing procrastination is a relatively straightforward one. However, it is comprised of numerous steps that must be followed in a particular order and to their fullest. What causes most people to fall short when it comes to overcoming procrastination is that they simply jump in and perform a few steps at random without any rhyme or reason. In a way, this would be like trying to bake a cake without following the recipe. Even if you use the right ingredients, unless you perform the steps in their proper order, you will fail to create anything worthwhile. However, when you use the right ingredients and follow each and every step carefully, you will create a perfect, delicious cake. Likewise, when you follow the steps for overcoming procrastination in their precise order, you will give yourself the best possible chance for success, enabling you to overcome procrastination once and for all. This chapter will address the various steps, providing a brief overview that will be elaborated upon in further chapters. By understanding the nature and order of these steps, you will be able to take control of your life and start achieving the success you so desperately desire.

Understand Your Reasons for Procrastinating

The first step to overcoming procrastination is to understand the reasons for your procrastination in the first place. This can be likened to you trying to find a cure for insomnia. Simply knowing that you are sleep deprived isn't enough when it comes to solving the problem. After all, there are numerous reasons for sleep deprivation, including not setting aside enough time for sleep, sleeping in a bright room, too much noise, a bad mattress, or high levels of stress and anxiety. Changing your mattress won't cure your lack of sleep if you aren't setting aside enough time to sleep each and every night. Nor would taking supplements help if you slept in a loud and bright room. Only when you identify the cause of your sleep deprivation can you take the proper steps to overcome it. Thus, if you knew you had a bad mattress, then replacing it would ensure you got better sleep, as would adding more time each night if that were needed.

This is how overcoming procrastination needs to be addressed. While you might get lucky if you simply jump in and start trying all of the methods randomly, the chances are you will only experience nominal results. This will probably cause you to fall short of creating any lasting and effective habits, as you won't get the results you need. However, when you take the time to carefully examine the true nature of your procrastination, you will be able to identify specific causes, each of which has a unique cure. By applying the cures that address your specific issues, you can ensure success in overcoming procrastination once and for all.

The first few chapters of this book cover the process of discovering the true nature of your procrastination, including whether it is behavioral or the result of your personality. No matter the cause, there is a guaranteed method or approach that will help you to change your behavior, and thus create a more productive life, one that allows you to achieve success on a regular basis. It is vital, however, that you take the time to carefully examine your situation. This is also true in the event that you try a particular method that proves less effective than you expect. Sometimes procrastination can have more than one cause, so if one cure only provides slight relief, the trick is to reevaluate your situation and look for other potential causes. Writing down your thoughts, efforts, and results in a journal, is a sure way to increase your chances of success. This will allow you to track your progress, noting which methods worked better and which ones failed to achieve the results you hoped for.

Identify Any Negative Thoughts and Change Them

One of the most common causes of procrastination is a negative mindset. This stands to reason, as the expectation of pain or pleasure can influence a person's behavior. If you tell a child that if they get their homework done, you will take them to get some ice cream, they will work like a maniac in order to get their reward. However, if you tell the same child that when they finish their homework, you will let them mow the lawn, suddenly the incentive to get their work done disappears. This isn't laziness, nor is it some self-destructive mindset that keeps the child from achieving success. Instead, it is a matter of stimulus. Positive rewards will encourage a person to pursue the goal that provides those rewards, whereas a lack of reward, or even worse, a painful outcome will cause a person to delay or even avoid the goals that lead to those less desirable outcomes.

Unfortunately, many of the undesirable outcomes that people predict are self-created. Failure, for example, is never guaranteed. Yet, most procrastinators have it in their mind that the task or project at hand will somehow lead to failure, thereby causing them negative results. This causes them to delay or avoid those tasks and projects, which ultimately leads to the failure they were afraid of in the first place. The trick is to identify any negative thoughts and to change them, thereby creating a more positive mindset in the process. In the case of the fear of failure, you would take the vision of failing and replace it with one of actually achieving the goal at hand. Thus, rather than having your mind filled with images of ridicule and embarrassment, you would fill your mind with images of happiness, validation, and even praise from your peers. This is how you remove the negative expectation that causes procrastination, and replace it with a positive expectation, one that encourages action and gives you all the inspiration you need to accomplish any task or project.

Confront Laziness

Another significant cause of procrastination is laziness. What sets this cause apart from all others is that laziness is a personality trait, not a behavior. Therefore, procrastination caused by laziness isn't as simple to fix as procrastination caused by disorganization. Instead, it will take a great deal more time and effort to get a handle on, to begin to change in a real and meaningful way. Fortunately, the steps for achieving this goal are proven and relatively straightforward. The key is to follow them precisely and to commit to them for as long as it takes.

In order to understand laziness and how it can be cured, it is necessary to understand the relationship between personality and behavior. Any behavior can be learned, which means that any bad behavior can be unlearned and replaced with a better one. However, this is only true in the case of behaviors not associated with personality. In the case of those directly influenced by personality, it isn't enough to simply change the behavior. Instead, you need to take the necessary steps to change your personality at its core, thereby changing all of your behaviors in the process because personality directly influences behavior.

Fortunately, although the process of changing your personality will require time and effort, it is fairly straight forward in nature. Simply put, the trick is to turn the equation around. Thus, instead of letting your personality affect your behavior, you start letting your behavior influence your personality. By engaging in more positive behavior on a grand scale, you can virtually rewrite how your mind works, changing everything from how you perceive work to how you perceive life itself. Therefore, once you start to exchange bad behaviors for good ones, you will start to notice a shift in how you think and feel overall. This shift will continue as you practice better behaviors and habits until, eventually, your personality will have evolved. Eventually, you will replace laziness with a sense of purpose, and this new personality will influence all of your choices and behaviors, helping you to live a better life in every possible way.

Organize Your Life

Chaos is another element that keeps countless people from fulfilling their full potential and thus achieving the success they deserve. This can come in several different ways, including a chaotic schedule, a chaotic work environment, and even a chaotic state of mind. More often than not, one manifestation of chaos will lead to the others, meaning that a chaotic schedule can spill over into a chaotic work environment and mindset. Fortunately, the reverse is also true, meaning that when you start to eliminate chaos in one area, you find that the other areas follow suit.

The simplest way to overcome chaos is to organize your life. Whether you choose to do this from the outside in, or the inside out, doesn't matter as such. What matters the most is that you approach this in the way that works best for you. Thus, you might choose to address your workspace, clearing the clutter, and organizing the things that need to remain. As you master the art of organizing your physical space, you will begin to notice that your thoughts, emotions, and other non-physical elements also become better organized. Eventually, you will regain control over your life, eliminating chaos and all the negative consequences it brings.

One such consequence is procrastination. The fact is that a lack of organization can cause even the most dedicated and hard-working person to put off tasks and projects until a better time. Unfortunately, that better time rarely comes. However, once the individual restores order to their life, both in physical and non-physical terms, then their tendency to procrastinate will virtually disappear, along with the chaos and confusion that plagued them. The dynamic for organizing your life is very similar to that of overcoming laziness, in that bringing organization to your behaviors and actions will, in turn, bring organization to your personality. This will begin to influence all of your behaviors in a positive way, removing the blocks that keep you from achieving your full potential.

Break Down Large Projects into Smaller Tasks

Most causes of procrastination stem from the individual in question. This is true when the cause is due to behavior or personality. Laziness, a disorganized lifestyle, and even the fear of failure, are all part of the individual rather than the circumstances they face. However, there are times when procrastination is the result of the task or project at hand, rather than anything to do with the person facing that task or project. In such a case, the way to overcome procrastination is to change the nature of the task or project, not to change the individual. Fortunately, this process is one of the easiest to perform, and it usually requires little more than a fresh approach, which turns even the most daunting project into something desirable and easy to achieve.

One of the best examples of this is to break down large projects into smaller tasks. Sometimes what causes a person to put off a project is the sheer size of the undertaking. Such things as painting a house or building a deck can seem far too complex, making even the most honest and hardworking person put off the project for as long as possible. Most of the time, a person will put off a large project because they lack the time or energy to complete the entire job. The idea is that they might have more time or energy later on down the road. Unfortunately, this is rarely the case. More often than not, the amount of time and energy you have available now is the same amount that you will have in the future. Therefore, the trick is not to make your resources grow, but to make your project shrink. When you break down a large project into smaller, more manageable tasks, you make it possible to accomplish each smaller task with the time and energy you have at your disposal. Eventually, as you knock out one task after another, you begin to accomplish the big project as a whole. Additionally, you will be less likely to avoid the smaller tasks, thereby eliminating procrastination once and for all.

Create Good Habits

The final step to overcoming procrastination is to create good habits. This makes a whole lot of sense when you consider that most forms of procrastination are the result of bad habits and behaviors in the first place. Whether those bad habits are the consequence of laziness, poor time management, low self-esteem, or any similar condition, the bottom line is that once they are replaced with better habits, the negative consequences will be replaced with positive results. In the end, a person's actions are what defines them, not their thoughts, or even their personality. Subsequently, by creating good habits, you achieve greater success and begin to live the life of your dreams.

One of the most critical elements in the creation of good habits is to keep a journal. This will enable you to do three things. First, it will enable you to write down the challenges you face. Once you have your "demons" down on paper, you will begin to feel more in control of your life right away. This will give you the courage needed to face those demons and to begin improving your habits, and thus your life. The second thing is that it enables you to write down the changes you want to make. Thus, if your bad habit is to oversleep, your desired change might be to go to bed earlier, or to simply get up the first time your alarm goes off. Writing this down will help you to commit to the solution, thereby increasing your chances of success. The third thing a journal enables you to do is to track your progress. If your initial efforts fall short, you can see why, and this will help you to make changes that will improve your results. Therefore, if you are serious about overcoming procrastination once and for all, it is essential that you keep a journal in which you record every aspect of your journey.

The best thing about creating good habits is that those habits will begin to improve who you are as a person. As mentioned earlier, personality directly influences behavior. That said, behavior can also directly affect personality. Therefore, each and every good habit you form will improve your personality in some unique way. The more good habits you create, the greater that improvement will become. Eventually, not only will you have achieved your goal of overcoming procrastination, you will also have achieved an element of personal development that will affect every area of your life. This will lead not just to greater productivity but also to higher self-esteem, a more positive mindset, and a general sense of self-confidence, which will enable you to chase after those goals that help you turn your life into the life of your dreams.

Chapter 5: Tweaking Your Thoughts to Avoid Procrastination

The human mind is nothing short of a miracle. Capable of conceiving everything from art to technology, the power of the mind is quite literally beyond measure. Interestingly enough, in addition to creating art and technology, the human mind also creates the way a person sees the world around them. In a way, it could be said that the mind creates reality itself. Thus, if a person's mind is positive in nature, then the result will be that their reality, or at least their perception of reality, will also be positive. In contrast, when a person has a negative mindset, then their perception of reality becomes negative, resulting in depression, anxiety, and a greater tendency toward procrastination. While this might appear to be a fixed situation, and one that cannot be changed in any significant way, the truth of the matter is that a person's mindset can virtually be programmed in any direction, positive or negative. This chapter will explore the impact thoughts have on procrastination, as well as the methods for changing those thoughts, thereby creating a mindset that avoids procrastination altogether.

The Chemistry of Success/Failure

When you think of the human brain, you probably think of a solid, gray mass that resides in your head. While this is true to a degree, the fact is that the brain is far more complex than it appears. Rather than just being a large lump of gray matter, your brain is a bio-electric computer of sorts. Electrical impulses are constantly firing throughout your brain, sending everything—including signals, thoughts, memories, feelings, and even desires—throughout your body and mind. The problem is that most people believe that the state of their brain is relatively fixed, in that how they think, feel, or perceive reality is unchangeable, much like the color of their eyes or the number of fingers they have. However, the reality is that the brain can be literally programmed, much the way any computer or computerized device can be programmed. All it takes is a little understanding of how the brain works and a little effort to change its current way of thinking.

The first thing to understand is how repetition affects your very mindset. Neuroscience has shown that the brain contains synapses: these synapses are like fingers that fire out electrical impulses that release chemicals into the body. A good way to envision this is to take your hands and place your fingers together. Then move your fingers apart a couple of inches, maintaining their alignment. The synapses in your brain don't actually touch, instead they face each other, like your fingers, and shoot electrical impulses across space in between, space known as the "synaptic cleft." When one synapse fires an electrical impulse into the other, the receiving synapse sends that impulse to a part of the brain that creates a chemical reaction. This is how positive thoughts create positive feelings, and negative thoughts create negative feelings.

What most people don't know is the fact that since the synapses aren't connected, they can be realigned. This means that the alignment that allows for negativity can be changed, creating an alignment that allows for positivity. Known as "neuroplasticity," this is the malleable condition of the brain. Therefore, rather than being a victim of your thoughts and feelings, you can actually rewrite how your brain works, changing the very nature of your thoughts and feelings in the process. Needless to say, this process is a gradual one, requiring a great deal of effort and time. However, just like lifting weights, if you put in the time and effort, the results will follow. The trick is to tweak your thoughts from those of a negative mindset to those of a positive mindset; one filled with hope, optimism, and inspiration.

The final thing to understand is why it seems as though your particular mindset is natural. In addition to forming alignments, synapses can also move closer together over time. Although they will never touch, the distance an electrical impulse has to cover—moving from one synapse to another—can shrink over time. This is due to repetition. The more you think a particular thought, the easier that thought becomes. Therefore, if you constantly think about failure, the synapses responsible for that thought and the fear that accompanies it will move closer and closer together, making those thoughts more readily available. However, this applies to a positive mindset, as well. Once you successfully reprogram your mind, you will create the neurological pathways that allow you to have positive thoughts and feelings quickly and easily. In a way, it's a bit like programming shortcuts to sites on the Internet. Rather than having to take the time to navigate to a site, you simply push one button, and you are there. This is how thoughts work in the brain. Once you create those shortcuts, you make that way of thinking easy and natural.

Change Your Perspective

The reason this is important is that the nature of your mindset will directly affect your decision-making process. Needless to say, a big part of that process is deciding when to address the tasks and projects at hand. If you have a negative mindset, you will be far more likely to procrastinate than if your mindset is positive in nature. Therefore, being able to reprogram your mind is essential if you want to be able to change your habits in a significant and lasting way. In short, the best way to change your behaviors is to change your perspective. Once you change your perspective, your habits and behaviors will change largely on their own, requiring very little effort on your part.

The first step to changing your perspective is to change the alignment of your synapses. While this sounds like something only a neurosurgeon can do, the fact is that anyone can accomplish this goal. The trick is to begin thinking in a different direction. For example, if you find that you constantly focus on the likelihood of failing at any task you perform, start imagining yourself succeeding instead. Take the time to replace the vision of falling short with one of being successful. Picture yourself handing in the project on time, or even better, ahead of schedule. Instead of imagining your boss ridiculing you for inferior work, picture them praising you for a job well done. Create the reality you wish to experience, not the one you are afraid of, or the one you remember from past situations. This is how you change the formation of your synapses, causing you to create a positive mindset in which hope, optimism, and self-confidence begin to replace the fear of failure and low self-esteem that caused you to procrastinate in the first place.

The second step to changing your perspective is to change the distance of the synapses. As mentioned before, the closer the synapses are, the easier the thought processes become. The trick here is to create repetition. If you only think positive thoughts from time to time, the synapses will remain further apart, allowing them to realign more easily back into their previous, negative alignment. However, if you take the time and effort to think positive thoughts all through the day, you will shrink the synaptic cleft, making your positive mindset easier to access and easier to maintain. A good way to achieve this goal is to create a list of five positive questions that you ask yourself at least three times a day. You can choose to ask these questions first thing in the morning, when you are having lunch, and last thing at night. Adding more times during the day will only increase your results, giving you faster and more significant success. A good set of questions to ask include the following:

- What can I be grateful for today?
- What will bring me happiness today?
- How can I flirt with someone I am interested in today?
- How is today better than yesterday?
- What can I do to be my best self today?

When you ask these questions, you begin to shift your focus from any negative thoughts to more positive, upbeat thoughts. This will help to create a positive mindset, one that brings happiness, confidence, and purpose to your day-to-day life. The more you ask these questions, the more you will change the way your brain functions. In as little as thirty days, your mindset will have been altered significantly. Another thirty days will see your mindset established, making your newly created positivity the new way you think each and every day.

Another way to change your way of thinking is to change your perspective on who you are. This can be done much the same way as changing your thoughts. In this case, you will write down three words that describe your ideal self, the person you ultimately want to be. These three words can be anything at all, and they can change over time as you begin to move forward in the direction of self-improvement. The trick is to repeat these words all throughout the day, making them the mantra of your improved self. Words such as exciting, happy, optimistic, gracious, confident, charming, commanding, inspiring, determined, and the like, can form your mantra. The important thing is to choose words that strike a chord, words that inspire you to be your best. Once you have your words, repeat them as often as you can, including when you wake up, when you go to bed, and all throughout the day. You can recite them when driving to work, standing in line at the grocery store, or even riding an elevator. The more you recite your words, the more your mind will identify with them, changing your sense of self, transforming you into the person you most want to be.

Change the Vernacular

The previous sections have focused on how to change your mindset, thereby changing how you think and how you perceive yourself. By replacing a negative mindset full of fear, dread, and self-loathing with a positive mindset full of hope, excitement, and confidence, you can remove the very causes of procrastination from within. The result is that your behaviors and habits will change automatically, giving you all the tools you need to achieve the success you have always dreamed of. However, there is another way in which you can change your perspective on things, one that reprograms your mind by changing the very definition of the tasks or projects at hand. This is the process of "changing the vernacular."

Many examples of this process can be seen in day-to-day life, especially in terms of specific jobs and their descriptions. At one time, a person who collected trash was known as a garbage man, whereas today, they are referred to as a "sanitation engineer." Maids are now known as housekeepers or domestic assistants. Secretaries are now personal assistants. Janitors are now custodians, and the list goes on and on. The reason for these title changes was to improve the image of the job at hand. Title changes resulted in a higher sense of self-esteem within those performing the jobs, as well as an increased number of people applying to fill the needed positions. In the end, even though the job itself didn't change by changing the title, it took on a more positive sounding tone. This is precisely how you can change your perspective on the tasks and projects you face each and every day.

More often than not, the things you procrastinate on are those things you dread doing. For example, if you hate washing dishes, then you will put off washing dishes for as long as you can. The very sound of those words will be enough to make you shudder and find any excuse to avoid facing the task. However, by changing the name of the task, you can change the very tone of it as well. Instead of calling the task "washing dishes," you can call it "preparing to make dinner," or "beautifying the kitchen." Although the task itself hasn't changed, if you focus on a different element, such as the desired result, or another task that is more pleasant, then you become less likely to procrastinate as your motivation is increased. Everyone likes to eat dinner, and everyone enjoys a beautiful kitchen. Therefore, focusing on those elements can be enough to change your perspective completely, removing the desire to procrastinate as a result.

This can be done for even the most fear-inspiring tasks as well. Public speaking, for example, is something that most people dread, and thus they put off for as long as possible, reducing their chances of success in the process. The trick is to change your perception of the event by changing the event's name. Rather than calling it "public speaking" call it "impressing my boss," or "impressing the person I have a crush on." This takes the focus from the task and places it on a desirable outcome; one that might not even have anything to do with the task itself, such as in the case of impressing someone you have a crush on. Once you create this expectation, you shift how your mind perceives the task, giving you the incentive and optimism to face it head-on without delay.

Negativity as a Positive

One final thing to consider is that negative thoughts aren't always bad in and of themselves. The simple truth is that everyone has negative thoughts each and every day. This is due to the fact that the human brain is hard-wired to predict danger, thereby protecting the individual from as much harm as possible. Subsequently, having negative thoughts isn't the real problem. Rather, the problem is when you allow those thoughts to control your emotions and actions. The thoughts themselves can actually serve as a tool for success when you know how to use them correctly.

The first thing to do is to become aware of your negative thoughts. More often than not, people either try to suppress any negative thoughts that come their way, or they allow them to play in the background, like a radio constantly playing music that undermines self-confidence and self-esteem. However, when you take the time to recognize those thoughts and ask why they are there, you might just get some insights that will prove useful in the end. If, for example, you are afraid of failing at a task or project because you failed a similar task or project in the past, take the time to contemplate the reasons for your past failure. This will enable you to learn valuable lessons, ones that can keep you from making the same mistakes as before, thereby increasing your chances of success.

A good way to turn negative thoughts into tools for success is to create a checklist from them. If, for example, you are afraid of giving a speech in public, and the fear stems from the fact that your last public speaking event was a disaster, take the time to list out what went wrong the last time around. If you forgot your lines, write that down. If you experienced difficulty in speaking because your mouth dried up, write that down. If you tripped over your shoelaces, or the batteries in your laser pointer died, write that down. Carefully dissect the things that went wrong before and then create a checklist for your next event. This list will include such things as follows:

- Put fresh batteries in your laser pointer and have extras on hand.

- Drink water before your speech and have a glass of water on hand.

- Don't wear shoes with laces.

- Keep bullet points of your speech in view in case you get distracted.

Now, rather than simply suppressing your fear, you turn it into a helpful aid, one that ensures you are fully prepared for your next endeavor and that you will avoid the pitfalls that robbed you of success the last time around. Furthermore, tell yourself that success is the default result and that only a lack of preparation will keep you from achieving it. Now that you are better prepared, you can expect a better performance, one that will put the painful memories to rest and replace the negative perspective with a positive one. This is how you use your inherent fears to your advantage.

Chapter 6: Ten Proven Ways to Beat Laziness

Laziness is probably the hardest cause of procrastination to overcome. This is because it is more than a mere bad habit or behavior that needs to be changed. In essence, laziness is a personality trait, something that affects not only behavior but a person's outlook on life in general. Therefore, it usually takes more than a few tweaks to change behavior caused by laziness. Fortunately, there are several techniques that will enable a person to begin to address their lazy tendencies and create a more productive, positive mindset instead. This chapter will focus on ten such techniques, each proven to effectively address specific causes and symptoms of laziness. By implementing all or even just a few of the methods discussed in this chapter, even the "laziest" person can begin to affect meaningful and lasting change in their life.

Be Forgiving

One of the most important steps to overcoming laziness is to be forgiving. The simple truth is that laziness can be a vicious cycle, one started by a lazy thought or intention but perpetuated by guilt, depression, and a general feeling of low self-worth. More often than not, this impacts people who are aware of their laziness and want to overcome it. After all, those who are completely lazy and have no interest in changing their ways have no reason to feel guilty. However, when a person seeks to improve themselves but falls back into lazy habits, they can create a vicious cycle that keeps them from ever breaking free.

The only way to break out of such a cycle is to end the mindset of guilt. Rather than allowing guilt and regret to fill your mind, you need to be forgiving of yourself. Take the time to recognize that you are facing a significant struggle and that setbacks will happen. Give yourself permission to both let go of past mistakes and not take future mistakes to heart. Understand that the process will take time, but that as long as you stay in the race, eventually you will cross the finish line and create the change you are so desperate for. Any time you feel yourself slipping back into guilt and frustration, remember that you are not alone and that plenty of others struggle with the same issues you face. Therefore, you are not a bad person; rather, you are a good person who is simply trying to break bad habits.

Take the First Step

When it comes to addressing laziness on a day-to-day basis, few methods are as effective as taking the first step. This comes down to a matter of physics: creating momentum. Anyone familiar with physics knows that it takes the greatest amount of energy to set a still object into motion. Once that object is moving, it takes less energy to keep it moving. In fact, this is the first Law of Motion discovered by Isaac Newton. Simply put, when an object is at rest or in motion, it will remain so unless acted upon by another force. Thus, the hardest part is to go from still to moving. Once you get the proverbial ball rolling, everything suddenly becomes easier.

How this translates into productivity is quite simple. As long as you don't take the first step, the project or task at hand will remain at its most difficult level. However, once you take the first step, you set things into motion. Once in motion, it becomes easier to keep working than to stop, just as it was easier to stay still than to get moving. Therefore, all you need to do to overcome laziness when facing any task or project is to take that all-important first step. After that, each and every subsequent step becomes effortless, resulting in you achieving your goal before you realize it.

Begin Early

A big mistake many people make when it comes to addressing work of any kind is to leave it until later, for a time when they might feel more energized or motivated. The bottom line is that the longer you wait to start a task or project, the harder it becomes to ever get started. This is another example of the Law of Motion at work. Once you start delaying work, it becomes easier to keep delaying it. The more time that goes by, the more effort it takes to actually stop procrastinating and begin tackling the task at hand.

Needless to say, the best way to overcome this pitfall is to always begin working early. By starting right away, you avoid getting into the rut of putting work off for later. This actually makes it easier to get started, as you don't have any negative momentum to contend with. Instead, you only have to put in as much effort as it takes to get the ball rolling, then the rest will take care of itself. The fact of the matter is that everyone begins early; the only question is what direction they choose to go. Many choose to begin procrastinating, which makes their day harder as a result. Alternatively, those who begin working ensure that their day gets easier as it unfolds, removing the stress and fatigue that lead to further procrastination.

Take Plenty of Breaks

In the fast-paced environment of these modern times, a commonly held belief is that in order to be productive, you must always be working. Any time spent on anything, except work, is seen as time wasted. This is why lunch "hours" have been reduced to thirty-minutes in many cases, and shorter breaks have become all but non-existent in most workplace environments. However, instead of increasing productivity, a lack of downtime actually undermines a person's performance, resulting in less productivity and lower quality results. This is because a lack of downtime leads to the average person becoming burned out and thus ineffective at the task they are performing.

In order to avoid this situation, it is vital that you take plenty of breaks throughout the day. For some people, this might mean ten minutes every hour, whereas, for others, it might mean thirty minutes every couple of hours. The important thing is to find what works best for you and begin creating your schedule around that. Although it might seem counterintuitive to work less in order to get more done, the simple truth is that when your energy levels are restored, and your mind is refreshed, you perform at peak efficiency, making your efforts go further than if you are tired and overwhelmed. Too many people taking these breaks might appear to be lazy in nature; however, they actually help to prevent the lazy tendencies that come from fatigue, stress, and a general state of burnout as the result of working too hard for too long.

Eliminate Distractions

Laziness can have many different faces, making it hard to recognize at times, as it can appear to be something altogether different. A good example of this is the type of laziness that encourages a person to choose the more fun option rather than getting to work on the harder, more demanding tasks at hand. The problem here is that in an age of social media, cell phones, and constant access to the Internet, it can be all too easy to find things to do that are infinitely more fun than the work that needs to get done. A few minutes here and there can add up quickly, resulting in a day's productivity lost to an endless stream of distractions.

The best way to overcome this form of laziness is to eliminate distractions whenever possible. While turning off your cell phone may not be an option, especially if you receive work calls on your phone, or you use your phone for emergencies with loved ones, turning off notifications or even Internet access can make all the difference. Overall, the more distractions you eliminate, the fewer temptations you will face throughout the day, making it easier to stay focused on your work. Not only will this make you more productive, but it will also reduce errors made due to a lack of concentration.

Keep Your Motivation Refreshed

As already discussed, one of the main issues with laziness is that a truly lazy person sees work as a painful process. This means that instead of seeing a challenge or a chance to achieve success, they see hardship and drudgery, things that hardly inspire motivation. Since work has all the appearances of being painful and meaningless, it can be all too easy to avoid it at all costs. Fortunately, there is an easy trick, one that doesn't necessarily change the nature of work; rather, it shifts the focus of the individual in such a way as to keep their motivation refreshed. This is the trick of contemplating the downsides and upsides for achieving the task at hand.

For example, if you need to accomplish a difficult task before you are able to go home for the day, rather than focusing on the size and complexity of the project, you should focus on the reward of getting to go home once it is done. The longer it takes to accomplish, the longer you are stuck at work. Suddenly, instead of being painful, tackling the task at hand becomes desirable, as it directly relates to your ability to go home, put your feet up, and be as lazy as you want. Every task or project will have a reward associated with its completion, offering a way to keep your motivation refreshed no matter the situation.

Declutter Your Life

Another common cause of laziness is the sense of being constantly overwhelmed. This is usually the case when a person either has too many things to do at any given time or when their schedule isn't as organized as it should be. In either case, the simple solution to this scenario is to declutter your life. Just as you would declutter a workspace by getting rid of junk and unnecessary items, so too can you declutter your schedule by getting rid of unnecessary tasks and organizing what remains. Once you declutter your life, you will be less intimidated by the tasks and errands you need to do each day, enabling you to face your day with greater confidence and energy.

A good way to remove the unnecessary items from your daily to-do list is to sit down and ask which tasks are absolutely essential. Ask yourself if you only had a couple of hours to get things done, which things would you choose. When you know which items aren't important, you can remove them from your list, freeing up some time and energy and thus decluttering your schedule. While some of the things you remove might be able to be eliminated altogether, others might still have to be addressed. In this case, you can simply place them on another day, the way you would put unnecessary items elsewhere in order to clean up your workspace. Once your day is less overwhelming, you won't be so tempted to avoid it, thus eliminating the allure of lazy behavior.

Accept Setbacks

Any time you fear failure, it can be all too tempting to avoid tackling the harder, more daunting tasks, choosing instead to stick with easier tasks or no tasks at all. This goes back to the understanding that laziness is the result of a negative association with work, thus causing a person to avoid work at all costs. Therefore, the stronger your fear of failure, the more likely you are to become lazy in order to avoid facing your fears.

Needless to say, failure is something that cannot be avoided completely, no matter how hard a person tries. Instead, setbacks will come in many shapes and sizes. The trick here is to accept this fact and let go of the need to avoid failure in the first place. The bottom line is that even the best, most successful people experience failure in their lives. That said, failure is not anything to be ashamed of or to fear. After all, despite their failures, such people remain highly successful. Therefore, the only way forward is to let yourself off the hook when it comes to setbacks. You will face them from time to time, but they won't defeat you, nor will they define you. Instead, they will teach you valuable lessons that will enable you to become better and stronger. Once you realize this, you will be able to tackle any task or project, no longer worrying about the outcome.

Surround Yourself with Positive Energy

Whenever you spend time with a person, one thing you realize is that the energy of that person tends to affect your own energy. In other words, if you spend time with someone who is hyper and agitated, you will become agitated as well. The same holds true for depressed, uninspired people. When you spend time with anyone who has low motivation or who is lazy, you will begin to feel the same, regardless of your true nature. This becomes even more real in the event that you spend time in a crowd of people of the same mindset. Therefore, one sure way to overcome laziness is to stay as far away from lazy, low energy people as you can, surrounding yourself with positive, highly motivated people instead.

When you surround yourself with positive energy, that energy will begin to affect you the same way that negative or agitated energy will. This means that you will start to feel highly motivated, optimistic, and even eager to tackle any task or project you need to accomplish. Furthermore, by surrounding yourself with such people, you will create a support group. A support group provides constant encouragement that will enable you to be your best at all times. Any time you find yourself slipping back into bad habits or struggling to overcome lazy tendencies, the best thing to do is to find highly motivated people to spend time with, so that you can recharge your energy and restore your sense of inspiration.

Embrace Laziness

The final trick to overcoming laziness is to actually embrace laziness. This doesn't mean that you should be lazy all day, every day. Instead, it means that if you truly believe that you are lazy, then be as lazy as you want to be when the time is right. One of the problems that most people face when they try to overcome laziness is that they try to deny themselves the pleasure of being lazy altogether. Unfortunately, when you deprive yourself of something, it can cause you to desire it even more. Thus, if you try to be productive at all times, including on your days off and in your downtime, you might actually set yourself up for wanting to be lazier at work than ever before.

To avoid this pitfall, the trick is to put all your effort into doing the right thing at the right time. Thus, when you are at work, be as productive as possible, avoiding lazy behavior completely; however, once you get home and kick your shoes off, become completely lazy, getting your fill of downtime, rest, and general non-productivity. When you allow yourself to be totally lazy during your downtime, you won't need to get your fill when there is work to be done. In a way, it's just like sleep. When you get enough sleep at night, you don't feel tired during the day. Alternatively, if you are sleep-deprived, you struggle to stay awake during the day, since your body craves the sleep it lacks. This is how your mind works as well, craving what it lacks, even when the time isn't right. Therefore, by letting yourself be totally lazy when the time is right, you will be more productive when it's time to get to work.

Chapter 7: Plan it Out: Six Steps to Getting Things Done

For the past few decades, cookbooks have been one of the most successful niches in publishing. More and more cookbooks sell each year, creating a very profitable career for anyone with culinary skills. Although new and exciting recipes are the main reason for the constant sale of cookbooks, another commonly overlooked reason is the directions that go with those recipes. If the average person had to guess at how to make a meal, they would wind up making countless errors before figuring it out. Fortunately, the directions provided in cookbooks take out the guesswork, ensuring the person following the recipe gets the best results each and every time. This same approach can be used to eliminate the struggle and guesswork when it comes to doing anything in life, not just making dinner. When you come up with a clear, concise plan, you can ensure that your to-do list gets done completely and effectively each and every time, without the need to reinvent the wheel day in and day out. This chapter will discuss the value of planning things out, and how sticking to a well thought out plan can make all the difference when it comes to not only getting things done, but getting things done right.

Set SMART Goals

The first step to creating a plan is to establish the goal you want to achieve. Unfortunately, this step is usually the one most people rush through, if they even pay attention to it at all. The end result is that their efforts are scattered and ineffective, undermining their chances of success in a real and significant way. In order to maximize your chances of successfully achieving your goals, it is critical that you learn to set SMART goals; ones that structure your direction, effort, and time. The following steps will help you to set SMART goals in your life:

• Specific: whenever you set a goal, you need to make sure it is specific in every way. Simply saying you want to write a book, for example, is far too vague a goal to achieve. The trick here would be to decide the exact book you want to write, including the type of book, the word count, and even the title.

• Measurable: the next step to creating a SMART goal is to make the progress measurable. This breaks down all the necessary parts of the goal, turning the big project into smaller tasks. You might choose to set milestones for writing a set number of words per day or per week, establishing a momentum of sorts. As you check off each milestone, you can track your progress to the overall result you are striving for, namely writing your book.

• Attainable: while being clear and specific regarding your goals is critical, it is also very important to be realistic. If you are spread too thin with the responsibilities you currently have, or you aren't a very good writer, then you might need to rethink your decision. Therefore, always be sure that the goal you set for yourself is one that is achievable. This doesn't mean it has to be easy; rather, it simply means that it has to be possible.

• Relevant: another element to creating a SMART goal is the relevance of the goal itself. If you don't really want to write a book, there is no point in setting the goal as you won't care about accomplishing it. Therefore, you need to make sure that the goal you set is one that is inspiring and meaningful to you. This will help to keep you motivated, especially in the most difficult times.

• Time-bound: this is when you set a specific timeframe within which you want to write your book. Without that timeframe, you give yourself the opportunity to procrastinate indefinitely, putting off your dream until the "right time" comes. Therefore, in addition to choosing the goal you want, you will add that you want to get your book written by the end of the year. Furthermore, you need to add the time you will start putting your plan into motion, including timeframes within which to accomplish the specific milestones of your overall plan. This makes you more accountable in terms of time, thereby reducing the likelihood of procrastination.

Create the Right Environment

Once you have created a SMART goal for yourself, the next step is to create the right environment for accomplishing that goal. Simply putting in the time and effort isn't always enough to ensure that the job gets done. Instead, it is vital that you create the right environment, one that is designed to help you achieve your goal. After all, if you try to write your book while sitting on the sofa watching TV, the chances are you won't get much further than the title page. Therefore, once you decide on a goal, it is essential that you create an environment that will help you to focus on the task at hand, thereby giving you the best chance for success.

First and foremost, you need to eliminate any and all distractions. Removing distractions will help you to stay focused on the task at hand, which will increase your efficiency as well as the quality of your work. Additionally, a clean, organized environment has been proven to go a long way to reducing stress, increasing inspiration, and making any task more enjoyable overall. Therefore, take the time to create a space that is inviting, organized, and distraction-free. This will help you to get into the right frame of mind for getting any task or project done, no matter how large it might be.

Another way that you can create a better working environment is to play music in the background. Needless to say, different styles of music will create different mindsets, so it is important to find the one that suits your mood at the time, as well as one that helps you to focus and get your work done. While silence can prove good for some people, most people struggle to keep their minds focused on silent conditions. The end result is that their mind wanders, contemplating everything but the task at hand. When you play music in the background, it can have the effect of soothing your mind, thereby keeping it from being restless and wandering in every direction.

Another way to get your mind to focus on the task at hand is to meditate before you begin work. By taking as little as five minutes to sit and actively clear your mind, you can create a mindset that will be more focused on the present. Getting rid of the clutter and chaos in your mind is as important as getting rid of the clutter and chaos in your physical environment. In a way, this is the process of creating the right mental environment, one that helps you to be productive and efficient, thereby enabling you to accomplish all of your goals.

Set Some Easy Rules

As already mentioned, chaos plays a big role when it comes to procrastination. The more chaotic your environment, schedule, and mindset, the more likely you are to put things off, thereby reducing your chances of accomplishing your goals. Fortunately, if you create a few simple rules that you follow each and every day, not only can you eliminate most of the chaos from your life, you can prevent it from ever coming back. This will go a long way toward overcoming procrastination once and for all.

One easy rule to follow is what is known as the Two-Minute Rule. This simply means that any task that can be accomplished in two minutes or less should be addressed immediately. Although this may seem counterintuitive, especially with regard to focusing on one task at a time and avoiding distractions, the bottom line is that it will take as much time to write down or reschedule a two-minute task as it would to actually complete it. Therefore, rather than wasting extra time, or allowing those small tasks to add up, simply knock them out as they arise. This will keep your schedule free of clutter, thereby enabling you to stay on track when it comes to the larger tasks and projects.

Another easy, yet effective rule, is to write down any ideas as they come into your mind. Sometimes you might have an inspired thought as you are working on something, but rather than writing it down, you tuck it away in the back of your mind. This has the effect of splitting your attention. Now, instead of being wholly focused on the task at hand, you are also focused on remembering that important piece of information. The more ideas you tuck away in your mind, the more cluttered your mind becomes. In order to avoid this, always take the time to write random ideas down. This will keep your mind clear and focused, while also ensuring that you don't forget what might turn out to be a real breakthrough later on.

The final rule to apply to your day-to-day life is to keep your goals simple. For example, if you want to begin organizing your day each morning, rather than setting your alarm an hour earlier and forcing yourself to write a full itinerary, simply start with taking five minutes in the morning to write a shortlist of four or five things you want to accomplish. As you master the art of making your daily list you can move on to the next step, which might be spending five or ten minutes creating a schedule for the day. Once you master that step, you can add another, and so on. Instead of jumping into the proverbial deep end, take it gradually, one step at a time, keeping the goals simple, achievable, and fun.

Maintain Your Energy Levels

The importance of maintaining your energy levels cannot be overstated when it comes to accomplishing goals and achieving success in your day-to-day life. Unfortunately, this step is the one that most people skip over in order to scavenge time for other steps. The end result is that even though they might be doing everything else right, when their energy levels aren't at their highest, their results won't be as good as they might be otherwise. Therefore, it is absolutely essential that you keep your energy levels as high as possible at all times.

One way to do this is to take care of your body. Ensure that you get the right amount of sleep each and every night and that your sleep is of the right quality. Invest in a good mattress, make sure your room is totally dark, and eliminate as much noise as possible to create an environment where you will get good, restful sleep, which will recharge your batteries.

Another critical element when keeping your energy levels high is to eat right. Avoid foods heavy with sugar, salt, or fat, as these will only serve to drain your energy, not restore it. Instead, eat foods rich in vitamins, minerals, and protein, such as eggs, vegetables, beans, and fish. Even though it might take more time to make and eat a proper breakfast, the energy you get from that breakfast will make you far more productive all day long. In the end, your productivity will increase, despite the investment of time.

Avoiding burnout is another proven way to maintain your energy levels all throughout the day. The best way to achieve this goal is to schedule regular breaks throughout the day, ensuring you don't get bogged down in a task or project, which will drain you of your physical and mental energy. A good brisk walk for five minutes can make all the difference, getting your blood flowing, and raising your respiratory rate. Not only will this reinvigorate your body, but it will also help to clear and refresh your mind.

Set Yourself Up for Success

The next step that will help you to get things done each and every day is to set yourself up for success. This has a few aspects to it, each with its own impact on your ability to stay focused and to get things done. The first aspect is to create a daily plan. Many people choose to do this first thing in the morning as they are getting ready for work. While this may work for some, the fact is that the best time to create such a plan is actually the night before. This is because you can use your downtime at the end of the day to come up with the goals you want to achieve the next day, rather than forcing yourself to think in such specific terms right when you wake up. Take the time to list out the things you want to accomplish, as well as the desired timeframe. In short, write out a basic itinerary, one that will organize your day and keep you on track to accomplishing your goals.

Another aspect of this step is to reflect on your progress on a regular basis. When you simply put in the effort without taking the time to review how effective that effort is, you can get stuck in a rut, one that might not even help you to accomplish your goals. However, when you take the time to review your progress, including your successes and setbacks, then you can discover what efforts are beneficial and what efforts need to be replaced. The best time to do this is at the end of the day, when you can reflect on the events of the day and determine where you stand regarding the goals you want to achieve. In fact, this can segue into creating your itinerary for the next day, as you can determine the improvements and changes you need to make in real-time.

Find What Works for You

The final step that will help you to achieve your goals is to find what works for you. A big problem that many people face when trying to improve their lives is that they assume that what works for one person will work for them. Although all of the methods and techniques covered in this book are proven to be effective, the bottom line is that not all of them might be effective for you. Therefore, it is critical that you try each and every one in order to know which are useful and which just don't work for you.

A good example of this is with reviewing your day and creating an itinerary. As already mentioned, the ideal time to complete these tasks is at the end of the day. However, that might not actually be right for you. Instead, you might find that first thing in the morning is the best time for you. Perhaps you need to sleep on things in order to sort them out in your mind, finding meaning and answers that otherwise wouldn't be available. Or you might find that setting aside time in the middle of the day is best for you. In the end, it doesn't matter when you perform these tasks, what matters is that you use the tools that work for you in the best way possible.

Another example is meditation. Many people practice meditation in order to clear their minds, helping them to be calm and more focused. While this method is effective, it might not be right for everyone. If you are a highly energetic person, meditation might actually agitate you rather than calming and clearing your mind. In this case, you might need to engage in more energetic activity, such as kickboxing, running, or some similar exercise. This would help you to burn off excess energy, thereby relaxing you and clearing your mind. Thus, even though kickboxing and meditation seem completely different, they can, in fact, achieve the same goal. Therefore, the trick is to understand the fundamentals of self-improvement and discover the methods that help you to achieve them in your own life.

Chapter 8: How to Get Started on Any Project NOW

The analogy of momentum has already been discussed with regard to beating procrastination. Simply put, the hardest step in any journey is the first step. Once that all-important first step is taken, all the others tend to fall into place, requiring less and less effort as the momentum builds. That said, few things are as important to overcoming procrastination than finding the motivation and energy to get the ball rolling on any project or task. Fortunately, there are several tips and tricks that can help even the worst procrastinator to get started on the task at hand, thereby enabling them to accomplish anything they set their mind to. This chapter will discuss several of those tips and tricks, approaching the subject from all sides, including emotional, organizational, and social. By the time you finish reading this chapter, you will have all the tools you need to get started on any project *now*.

Get Excited

Few things make as much of a difference when it comes to productivity as excitement. The more excited you are about something, the more energy and enthusiasm you will have for getting that thing done. This can be seen each and every year when countless children all around the world wake up at the crack of dawn on Christmas morning. Compare that to the countless times the average child struggles to get out of bed on a school day, or on any day when chores, doctor's visits, and the like await them. The simple lesson here is that the average child isn't lazy or sleep-deprived, rather they are simply unmotivated when it comes to facing the days of drudgery. Alternatively, when an exciting day awaits, their energy levels soar through the roof. This phenomenon isn't restricted to young people; instead, it affects the hearts and minds of people of all ages.

With this in mind, the trick to getting started on something is to get excited about it. In a way, you need to treat the task or project like Christmas Day itself, promising all sorts of rewards and prizes. One of the best ways to achieve this goal is to create what is called a "vision board." Vision boards can be any kind of board, including a corkboard, dry erase board, or even a piece of poster board. The purpose of the board is to create a space where you can put all of the things that provide inspiration for your task or project. For example, if you need to paint your house and you are struggling to find the motivation, get a piece of poster board and fill it with pictures of painted rooms similar to the vision you have of how yours will look when it's done. The more you remind yourself of how wonderful the finished product will be, the more inspired you will be to get to work on making it happen.

More often than not, vision boards are used for long term projects or goals, things that will change your life in a real and significant way. An example of this would be losing weight. Perhaps you have struggled to start an exercise and diet regimen, keeping you from achieving your ambition of creating a healthier, slimmer you. Putting images of people you aspire to look like on a vision board will help you to keep your eyes on the proverbial prize, helping you to not only get started, but to also keep going even when times get tough. In addition to photos, you can put inspirational quotes, specific goals to keep you on track, and even images to track your progress, thus helping you to appreciate how well you are doing at all times. In the end, the most important thing is that the items on your vision board keep you motivated and excited, thereby encouraging you to put in the effort that will eventually allow you to achieve your goal and bask in the rewards that await.

Write it Down

Another proven way to help you get started on any task or project is to actually write your task or project down. Although this may not sound like much, it can actually make all the difference. The simple fact is that until you write down a goal, it remains nothing more than a pipedream, a fantasy that only exists in your mind. As a result, it never takes on any real form, making it easier to ignore, or even worse, forget about altogether. However, once you take that all-important step of putting your ideas down on paper, you take the fantasy and give it form, thereby giving it a reality. Now, instead of being just a dream, it becomes a vision, a goal, something your mind can now treat seriously because your eyes can see it in front of you.

Creating this visual quite literally shifts where your dream exists in your mind. As long as your dream remains a pure fantasy, it resides in your imagination. However, once you write down your dream, it becomes a problem to solve, thereby moving from your imagination to your intellect. Now your brain can start working on how to accomplish your goal, rather than using the image as an escape from reality. The important thing is to take the time to write out your dream in as much detail as possible, even listing all of the fears and concerns you have about turning that dream into reality. By putting everything down on paper, you literally jump-start your mind to figure out the solutions to all of those problems, thereby giving you the answers you need to get started on achieving that particular goal.

Needless to say, you don't want to write down your task or project in a way that focuses solely on the obstacles and challenges it presents. Although listing those things will help you to start solving them in your mind, the important thing is to also keep a positive spin on things, making sure you write down all the rewards of a successful outcome. Additionally, you can write down all of the negatives that would result from you not starting your project, providing the stick as well as the carrot when it comes to motivation. The simple truth of the matter is that such negative motivations can prove more influential than positive ones. Thus, they should be used to keep you inspired and motivated at all times. For example, if you want to look for a new job, you can use staying in your current job as negative motivation. List a few of the worst aspects of your job as a consequence of not working on achieving your goal and getting that better job. Furthermore, it is vital that you refer to this written goal as often as possible, at least a few times a day. This will keep it real in your mind and will keep you motivated to do whatever it takes to turn your dream into reality, thereby improving your life and achieving the happiness you deserve.

Commit Time to Your Project

One of the most common words used by the most successful people to explain how they achieve their success is: "commitment." No matter what the task or project might be, until you commit yourself to it, you will never put in the effort needed to accomplish your goal, and thus achieve the success you crave. The first element that you need to commit in order to get started on your task or project is time. After all, no amount of resources, inspiration, or energy will be of any use if you don't have the time needed to accomplish your goal. Therefore, before you try to find the tools and resources you need for your task or project, you must first set aside specific time to work on turning your goal into reality.

Unfortunately, this is where most people go wrong when it comes to starting a task or project, specifically a large one. More often than not, they wait until they have enough time to accomplish the entire task at once. Therefore, they only commit the time to the task when they have a large amount of time to spare. The trick is not to wait until you have large amounts of time. Instead, you should devote small portions of time to get started on the project. As little as fifteen minutes a day can be all that it takes to do any research on your project, acquire necessary resources, or even begin tackling the project in small doses. Thus, instead of waiting until you have enough time to do everything, simply set aside some of the time you do have in order to get as much done as you can.

The main side effect of this method is that it creates momentum. As you start working on your task or project, even for just fifteen minutes, suddenly, you crave more time so that you can get more done. The next thing you know, you are rearranging your schedule in order to find more time for the project that you had been procrastinating on for ages. Even if you can't find more time than the fifteen minutes a day, the bottom line is that those small doses will add up, as will the results of your efforts. After a couple of weeks, you will have spent a couple of hours on your project. That amount of time will put a huge dent into the overall process, giving you a head start at the very least. More often than not, those results add up sooner than you realize, seeing you accomplish your goal without ever having had to face it all at once. Therefore, no matter how little time you might have available, when you set aside a small amount of time each and every day, you will be able to achieve any task or project, no matter how large or complex.

Commit Resources to Your Project

Once you commit time to your task or project, the next step is to commit resources to it as well. This is another way that you take your dream and give it relevance in the material world. The simple act of purchasing the right equipment necessary to achieve your goal can make all the difference when it comes to taking the first step to getting that goal accomplished. A good example of this is with starting an exercise regimen. If you want to start running each and every day, once you set aside the time necessary for your run, the next step would be to acquire a good pair of running shoes and some comfortable athletic wear to go with them. The act of purchasing these items is an act of committing to the process, thereby making it more real in your mind. Being able to see and feel your running shoes makes your goal tangible, and that is all-important when it comes to getting started.

Sometimes a task or project may not need equipment as such, making this step appear more challenging as a result. The good thing is that no matter what the task or project is, it will always need resources of one form or another. For example, if you want to write a book, you might not need any extra equipment, especially if you already have a computer or laptop that you will use for your writing. In this case, you could create folders on your computer for finished documents. Additionally, you might set aside specific space within which to work. Creating space is a way of giving your goal life in the real world, especially if you don't use that space for anything else. Therefore, no matter how little your task or project requires in terms of resources, there will always be something you can do to bring your dream into the physical world, thereby making it more real and thus more necessary to get started on.

Another resource that almost all tasks and projects require is cold, hard cash. This is another way that you can commit resources and thus stop procrastinating once and for all. Although setting aside money in a savings account is a good option for a more expensive goal, such as going on a trip or doing home renovations, any time the amount of money needed is smaller, you can save it up physically. Using a glass jar to put money in not only sets money aside, but it also acts as a visible source of inspiration and motivation. Every time you put money in your jar, you know that you are moving closer to your goal. Additionally, just seeing the jar can keep your mind focused on the task at hand, giving you the motivation to get started as soon as possible. Thus, even though you might not be able to start the project until you have enough money saved up, by starting the process of setting aside the money, you will essentially have started the project, since you have begun the necessary preparations. In the end, it doesn't matter where or how you start. All that truly matters is that you do start, since once you have started, everything becomes easier as a result.

Create Incentives

The final trick to getting started on any task or project, no matter how large or complex, is to create incentives. Needless to say, such incentives can take many different shapes and forms, each depending on the nature of the task or project you are undertaking. For example, while treating yourself to your favorite ice cream, or a trip to your favorite burger joint may be the perfect reward for writing a chapter in your book or for making headway on a painting project, such a reward is ill-advised if your project is losing weight or starting an exercise regimen. Therefore, it is as important to pick the right reward as it is to create a reward in the first place. In the event you are trying to lose weight, you might choose to reward yourself with clothes shopping when you reach a specific target. Even a simple night out at the movies can go a long way to keeping you on track to reaching your goal.

Another incentive is that of creating accountability. When you are the only person who knows of your goals and dreams, it can be all too easy to put those goals and dreams off for another time. However, when your friends know as well, things suddenly change. Pride can go a long way to helping you stay true to your goals; therefore, it is always good to tell others of the things you want to accomplish. When you tell your friends, they will be sure to ask you about your progress each and every time they see you. Knowing this will keep you motivated to do your best so that you can give them a glowing report when they do ask. Additionally, friends can prove a valuable source of moral support, cheering you on when you need it the most. The positivity they can provide will help to keep your energy at its highest, enabling you to carry on even when you want to quit. Telling friends about a goal will ensure that you get started sooner rather than later, as they will hound you until you do. In the end, even though accountability isn't as nice as a reward, it can be as effective, if not more so when it comes to maintaining motivation and helping you to start that all-important project here and now.

Chapter 9: Bad Habits That Stifle Your Productivity (Plus Productivity Hacks)

Anyone who has ever started a diet, or a healthy life regimen will know that one of the most important aspects of achieving your goal is to break the bad habits and behaviors that are responsible for the situation you want to fix. In other words, before you even think about buying a good pair of running shoes or a mountain of green leafy vegetables, you must first throw away the containers of ice cream and the bags of chips. Only by eliminating the unhealthy foods in the first place can the other measures begin to take effect, helping you to become healthier and happier as a result. The very same thing applies to procrastination. In order for all the tips and tricks to produce the intended results, you must first remove all of the bad habits and behaviors that are keeping you from the success you desire. This chapter will address several of the most common bad habits that stifle your productivity, as well as ways to overcome them once and for all. By the time you finish reading this chapter, you will be able to clear the junk habits out of your life, thereby making way for the healthy, positive habits that will help you to fulfill your true potential.

Multitasking

One of the most common and harmful of all the bad habits regarding productivity is that of multitasking. This is an area where countless people make a critical mistake, one that keeps them from achieving the success they desire. That mistake is to start multiple tasks at once. Although multitasking might sound like you are more productive, the fact of the matter is that it decreases your productivity, making any task take longer to complete than if you had focused on that single task alone. There are actually a couple of reasons why this is the case.

First, there is simple math. If you start one task that will take ten minutes to complete, you can pretty much guarantee that you will get it done in ten minutes' time, provided you don't get distracted or called away. However, if you start five tasks that should only take ten minutes each, you suddenly have a different equation on your hands. Now, instead of getting the one task done in ten minutes, you probably won't get it done for thirty, forty, or even fifty minutes depending on how you split your time between the five different tasks. In the end, instead of speeding up when things get done, multitasking actually pushes back the deadlines, making it less efficient as a result. By focusing on one task at a time, you ensure that each task will be completed in ten minutes from being started, with the end result still being the same, namely getting all five tasks done in fifty minutes.

The second reason why it is better to focus on one task at a time is that you can devote all of your concentration to the task at hand. Numerous studies have shown that when you multitask, it causes your mind to become fragmented, juggling numerous tasks at once rather than simply focusing on one at a time. Furthermore, it has been discovered that the brain can't just go from one task to another seamlessly. Instead, it needs to gear down from one before gearing up for the other. Although it only takes a couple of minutes to switch gears, those minutes can add up over the course of a day, seriously undermining the efficiency of your time. The end result is that when you multitask, it actually takes longer to accomplish the same tasks than if you approached them individually. Therefore, always commit to one task at a time, putting all of your time, effort, and attention into it.

If you have five tasks to address the best approach is to prioritize them, placing the most important and time-sensitive one at the top of the list, while leaving the least important at the bottom. Once your list is made, you can begin performing each item individually, only going on to the next item when the first one is completed in its entirety. Taking a five-minute break between each task will help you to clear your mind and prepare for the next task at hand. Although it seems counter-intuitive in terms of productivity, such breaks will increase the speed and quality of your work, allowing you to produce better results than if you worked straight through. This will keep you organized, fresh, and motivated all throughout the day.

Constantly Focusing on the Big Picture

Another bad habit is that of constantly focusing on the "big picture." This is particularly true in the case of larger projects that require a lot of time and energy to accomplish. As already mentioned, such large projects can cause even the most energetic and hard-working people to procrastinate simply due to their size and scope. Only by breaking down those large projects can a person address them without feeling overwhelmed. However, sometimes it's hard not to remember the big picture, even after the large project has been broken down. This can cause a person to stumble in their progress, feeling overwhelmed, and losing their motivation to carry on.

This situation isn't necessarily the result of a lack of discipline or low self-esteem. Instead, it often happens when a person takes the time to track the progress they are making. The moment their mind leaves the small task at hand and sees the big picture, the feeling of being overwhelmed returns. They suddenly begin to regret taking on such a large project and start to doubt their ability to complete it.

Now, instead of being motivated and full of energy, the individual is demoralized and uninspired. These feelings usually cause them to procrastinate on the next step, resulting in the project going unfinished for an indefinite period of time.

Needless to say, contemplating the big picture in any project or task is a necessary step, especially when tracking your progress. The trick is to leave such contemplations for times when you aren't working on the project. In other words, rather than thinking about the big picture while you are working on a specific element of the project, take time at the end of the day to entertain those thoughts. Let your mind focus on the work you are doing while you are doing it and nothing more. This will help to keep you in the zone of the smaller, more manageable task. At the end of the day, you can look at the task as an observer, and this can help to keep you from feeling overwhelmed. Furthermore, by waiting until the end of the day to track your progress, you will always have more progress to show, helping you to stay motivated as you see the big picture getting smaller and smaller by the day.

Being Unstructured

Organization is another key ingredient to improving efficiency and thus increasing productivity. That said, one of the things that keeps most people from fulfilling their true potential is that they are unstructured. This can come in several different forms, including the lack of a work routine, a disorganized workspace, and even a disorganized mindset. In the end, a lack of organization serves to decrease both the amount and the quality of the work that is accomplished. No matter how much time or energy an individual puts into their work, the results will always be modest at best. In short, when a person lacks structure, they lack the direction needed to achieve their goals quickly and successfully.

The lack of a work routine is one of the most significant areas where being unstructured can really have a negative impact.

Numerous studies have shown that a person's energy levels fluctuate all throughout the day. Without a work routine, they may wind up sitting idle when their energy levels are at their peak, only to begin tackling the day's tasks when their energy levels are lower, causing them to be less productive as a result. The trick here is to pay attention to when your energy levels are highest, setting aside those times to tackle the hardest, largest tasks during the day. This will ensure that you use your time and energy as efficiently as possible, making you not only more productive but also more motivated, as you will only face demanding tasks when you are full of physical and mental energy.

The same applies to your workspace and mindset. Whenever you have disorganization, it can lead to confusion, time-wasting, and even a lack of inspiration. However, if you take the time to organize your workspace, making it easy to find all of the tools you need for the work you need to do, then you will be able to be more productive as a result. This applies to your mindset, as well. It is critical that you always focus your thoughts and attention on the task at hand. Allowing your mind to wander while you are working not only slows down productivity, it also increases the chances of making costly mistakes that will only make your work even harder. However, when you organize your thoughts, only recognizing those relevant to your work, then you will have a clean and organized mind, one that will be as useful and beneficial as your clean and organized workspace.

Striving for Perfection

Although a seemingly positive concept, perfection can actually prove more harmful than helpful when it comes to productivity. Mainly because our mind will always fixate on the things that can and do go wrong. As a result, the more you focus on perfection, the less likely you are to get anything done. Instead, you will constantly spend your time trying to avoid imperfections or dealing with the imperfections that occur. Since the idea of perfection rarely translates into the real world, it is unlikely that you will achieve perfection no matter how hard you strive to do so.

The inability to achieve perfection can be enough to keep you from getting started on a task if perfection is your aim. The more potential problems you see, the more likely you are to delay or avoid starting a task or project altogether. In the event that you do get started, you will be more likely to quit a project once it becomes clear that achieving a perfect result is beyond reach. Additionally, the stress and fatigue of maintaining unrealistic work standards may prove more than you can handle, causing you to metaphorically "work yourself to death" on a project that would have proven relatively easy otherwise.

Since perfection is a myth, at best, the trick is to not actually waste your time and energy trying to achieve the impossible. Instead, you should focus your attention on finishing each and every task or project you have. The bottom line is that a fully completed project is better than any half-completed one. Even if the half-completed one is perfect, it is still incomplete. In contrast, the finished project is done, meaning it has far greater value despite any flaws or imperfections. If a challenge is what you need, then rather than perfection, try focusing on finishing every task or project ahead of schedule. This will give you that competitive fix while still allowing you to be more productive.

Being Overbooked

Almost everyone feels as though they have more work to do in a given day than they have the time needed to get that work done. While this can prove unavoidable in some cases, more often than not, it is the consequence of another bad habit, specifically, the habit of never saying "no." Most people feel that turning down a request for help or an additional task will somehow appear as a sign of weakness, showing an inability to rise to the challenge. The fear of saying no causes them to constantly take on more and more work, so much so that they wind up getting overbooked. In the end, projects are either late or ignored altogether, making this a vicious cycle that leads to a lack of productivity and the low self-esteem that comes as a result.

The best way to avoid being overbooked is to learn to say "no." Although others may take such a rejection hard at first when you demonstrate your reasons, they will likely come to see the logic behind your decision. Alternatively, instead of simply saying 'no' outright, you might offer to make yourself available once your current task or project is complete. This will help you to put your work first while still proving useful to others when you have the time and energy to spare.

Another highly valuable trick is to schedule time within each and every day to take on additional tasks. Most people fill every single minute of their schedule with work or obligations, allowing no time for extra tasks or tasks that take longer than expected. If you schedule an empty half an hour in the middle or end of your workday, you can either give yourself that extra time for tasks that remain unfinished, or you can devote it to any tasks you take on in an effort to help others. This will ensure that the time you give never undermines your own productivity, thereby eliminating the scenario of being overbooked.

Waiting for Better Conditions

Finally, there is the bad habit of waiting for better conditions. How many times have you put off a task or project because you didn't feel as though you had the right amount of time or energy on hand? This happens to everyone, all of the time. Unfortunately, the right time rarely ever comes, meaning that you keep pushing back a task indefinitely. The same holds true with regard to energy levels. The amount of energy you have today will likely be the same amount of energy you have tomorrow, the next day, and the next day after that. This means that if now isn't the right time, the chances are the right time doesn't actually exist.

In order to break this habit, you need to change the order of things. Rather than shaping your time and energy to the task or project at hand, shape the task or project to the time and energy available. In other words, rather than putting off the entire task for later, simply accomplish as much as you can with the resources you have. Even if you only have ten minutes to spare, and your energy levels are at fifty percent, you will be able to get something done, thereby making more progress than if you did nothing at all. Needless to say, a large task or project may take a while to complete in such circumstances, but at the end of the day, it will get completed, and that's really all that matters. This is how you avoid building that list of huge projects that never get done. By switching things around, you will get every task and project done, no matter how large or labor-intensive they may be.

Chapter 10: The Success Mindset: Five Tips from Success Experts

When it comes to overcoming procrastination, all of the top experts agree on one fundamental truth: change comes from within. Although the methods for overcoming procrastination will help anyone who puts them into practice, in order to achieve true success, it is critical that you change your very way of thinking. The simple fact is that procrastination is usually the result of a failure mindset, the state of mind that focuses on problems, fear of failure, and all the other negative aspects of any endeavor. Alternatively, ambition, inspiration, and a desire to take action are the result of a success mindset, one that is focused on opportunities, dreams, and the rewards that await when goals are achieved. Therefore, in addition to practicing effective time management, organizing your life, and redefining challenges, it is essential that you develop a success mindset in order to realize your full potential and achieve the success you truly crave. This chapter will reveal five proven ways to develop a success mindset, thereby enabling you to overcome procrastination and every other obstacle that has been holding you back from the life you both desire and deserve.

Define Success

One of the most puzzling things to many people is when a seemingly successful person is unhappy with their life. They might have a dream job, a dream house, and the sort of financial security that most people only ever fantasize about, yet in spite of it all, they are still unhappy. To the average person, this might appear to be a sign that they are ungrateful for what they have, that they are unsatisfied with the gains they have achieved. However, the truth of the matter is that they are unhappy because the success they have achieved is not their version of success. Instead, they have achieved what society defines as success. This is where "defining success" plays a crucial role.

In order to be truly successful, you need to decide what success means for you. If it means financial security and all the luxuries that go with it, then pursuing a high paying job may be the path for you to follow. However, success for you might mean freedom, the freedom to do what you want, when you want. Since a high paying job will not afford that kind of freedom, you will need to find another path that will help you to achieve your goal. In the end, chasing after someone else's dream won't bring you happiness. Only when you pursue your dream will you achieve the happy, content life that you desire. Therefore, the first step to creating a success mindset is to sit down and write out the things you want most in life. These are the things that define success for you, and thus they are the things you should pursue in your efforts to turn your dreams into reality.

The next step to defining success is to resolve any inner conflicts that might interfere with the pursuit of your dream. For example, you might dream of getting a high paying job and all the financial stability that comes with it, yet you are afraid that you will sacrifice a happy, loving marriage in the process. This might cause you to drag your feet when it comes to chasing after that dream job. In this case, you need to decide that you can achieve both elements of your dream. By deciding that you will never let your job control your life, you can pursue a path of financial success, while still chasing after love and happiness at home. By addressing the fears and concerns of success, you can take control of your decisions, thus ensuring you achieve true, all-around success.

The final step is to translate your dream into goals. It's not enough to simply decide you want financial security. Instead, you need to determine how to go about achieving that dream. Will you find a high paying job, start a successful business, or make investments that will create your fortune? Needless to say, every destination has many roads leading to it, each from a different angle and perspective. Only by choosing one of these roads can you begin moving in the direction of your dream. Setting goals, both large and small, will help you to lay out a travel plan that you can monitor, thereby tracking your progress and ensuring that your actions and decisions lead you closer to your goal, rather than further away from it.

Create a Growth Mindset

When it comes to creating a success mindset, another factor to take into account is the danger of having a fixed way of thinking. A fixed mindset is when you have a rigid set of beliefs that cannot be changed or altered in any way. More often than not, this fixed set of beliefs includes the things that you consider impossible, faults you feel are a part of your natural condition, and any number of negative aspects that keep you from pursuing your dreams and fulfilling your potential. In contrast, the most successful people create what is known as a growth mindset, one that is capable of changing, evolving, and growing with each and every experience, thereby allowing for the individual to develop their abilities and strengths.

One of the most effective ways to create a growth mindset is to constantly challenge yourself to improve. This is a good way to turn setbacks into learning experiences. Each and every time you experience a setback, rather than admitting defeat, take a look at where you went wrong and determine never to make the same mistakes again. When you achieve this mindset, you eliminate the fear of failure completely from your life, since failure becomes a chance to grow and improve, thereby helping you to hone your skills and pursue your dreams more effectively.

Although failure is a good way to challenge yourself to improve, the most successful people take it a step further and use their successes to challenge growth and development as well. Rather than sitting back and basking in victory, successful people look at their wins and ask how they could have done even better. This constant desire for self-improvement forces you to continually strive to be your best. Even if you fall short of this goal, you will still continue to grow, becoming better with each day and each experience. The trick is to appreciate your achievements, while also looking for ways to make those achievements even better.

Another significant difference between a fixed mindset and a growth mindset is the ability to embrace change. Since change challenges your comfort zone, if you have a fixed mindset, you will resist it at all costs. This means you will never push beyond your accepted limits, resulting in modest levels of success at best. Alternatively, when you have a growth mindset, you will see change as a chance to grow and experience new horizons, horizons that offer fresh opportunities and higher levels of success. By embracing change, not only do you grow, your dreams grow as well, meaning the success you gain by achieving those dreams will be larger than you ever imagined. This growth mindset will take away the fear of the unknown, and thus remove any tendencies toward procrastination that results from such fears.

Become Self-Aware

While the saying: "ignorance is bliss" may be true for some, the fact is that ignorance is usually the cause of failure for most people. This is because the more ignorant you are, the less you know, and the less you know, the less likely you will be to succeed. Knowledge is power, and the most important and powerful of all types of knowledge is that of self-awareness. Only by knowing yourself can you begin to create a success mindset, one that enables you to chase and fulfill all of your dreams and ambitions. Therefore, it is vital that you take the time and effort to become self-aware.

The first step toward becoming self-aware is to discover your weaknesses. This can be a hard process for many, since admitting to your weaknesses is often seen as the same as accepting them. However, the only way you can fix your weaknesses is to know what they are in the first place. Therefore, it is critical that you take the time to contemplate what areas you struggle with. These areas can include anything at all, like public speaking, embracing change, learning new skills, or anything that is outside your comfort zone. Once you discover your weaknesses, you can begin to do two things. First, you can begin to affect change in those areas, developing your skills so that you turn your weaknesses into strengths. The other thing is to make choices that don't expose your weaknesses. In other words, if you struggle with public speaking, then don't necessarily take a job that requires a lot of public speaking, at least not until you take the steps needed to overcome that particular weakness.

The next step is to discover your strengths. This will help you to know what skills you have in abundance, in order to make better decisions all around. If, for example, you are highly skilled at writing, then pursue any opportunity where you can put your writing to use. A big mistake that people make is in assuming that when you tailor your choices to your strengths and weaknesses, you limit your opportunities to those that fall within your comfort zone. In fact, when you tailor your choices in this way, you maximize your chances of success in everything you do. If you never pursue growth and development, then you will run the risk of becoming stagnant. However, you can find a healthy balance where you focus on your strengths, avoid your weaknesses, and continue to improve in all areas. This is one of the keys to achieving both short term and long-term success.

The final step to becoming self-aware is to discover and develop your intuition. Many people shy away from the idea of using intuition when it comes to making important decisions, as it takes away from a more intellectual approach, where data and experience are used to make the best choice. Unfortunately, data and experience aren't always available, meaning that there will be times when your "gut feeling" is your only source of inspiration. By taking the time to develop and listen to your intuition, you gain an advantage, one that allows you to make the best decision, even when there is no empirical data to use in the decision-making process. The trick is to listen to your intuition at all times. Recognize how you feel with each and every decision you make. This will help you to trust your intuition in those times when you have no other source of insight to follow.

Ignore the Opinions of Others

If you've ever listened to the story of a successful person, you will probably have heard them say how they pursued their dreams when others said it couldn't be done. Needless to say, had they paid attention to those negative opinions, they would never have chased their dreams, and thus would never have achieved the success that has since defined them. Therefore, when it comes to creating a success mindset, it is essential that you develop the ability to ignore the opinion of others.

One of the things you need to ignore right away is how others define "success." This goes back to the idea of defining what success means to you personally. All too often, people spend their time and energy pursuing what others perceive as success. Whether it's money, a prestigious job, or any similar common dream, if it's not what you really want, then it will never bring you the happiness you desire. Before you begin chasing a dream, you need to ask yourself who's dream it is that you are chasing. If it's not yours, then it's not right. When you spend your life chasing the dreams of others, you become a slave to their way of thinking. Thus, even if you achieve success, you never actually live your own life. Successful people ignore the vision of success that society shares, choosing to focus on their personal desires and goals, regardless of what others think. In the end, true success is living a life that brings you untold happiness, meaning, and contentment. The only way to achieve such a life is to shut out the vision of success that others hold and focus on your vision, your ambition, and your dreams.

The second opinion to ignore as soon as possible is that of the expectation of failure. Again, how many success stories start with the recollection of how countless people said it couldn't be done? Everything from crossing the ocean to flying to the moon came in spite of almost everyone claiming failure was all but certain. Imagine, for a moment, what the world would be like today had the early explorers and pioneers accepted common belief and simply stayed home, instead of reaching out and achieving greatness. The very same thing holds true for your life. If you allow the negative mindset of others to restrict your vision, then you will only ever achieve the success others can imagine. Alternatively, when you ignore what others say, you open up an infinite world of possibilities, enabling you to pursue any dream as long as you have the ability to envision it and the courage to do what it takes to turn it into reality. In other words, when others tell you that it can't be done, recognize that what they mean is that it can't be done by anyone other than you.

Interestingly enough, another opinion you need to dismiss is that regarding your true worth. It makes sense to ignore people when they tell you something is impossible, as their negativity can hold you back. However, the same thing can happen if you listen to positive people who tell you that you have what it takes to succeed. This isn't to say that you should ignore positive reinforcement completely, rather it means that you shouldn't limit yourself to how others perceive you. Sometimes when other people praise you and hold you in high esteem, it can undermine your willingness to take risks, in order to avoid falling short in their sight. This is what happens when you fall into the trap of upholding other people's expectations. In order to avoid this trap, you need to ignore the opinions of others and focus solely on your goals. Don't worry about how they might react, whether you succeed or fail. Instead, keep your eye on the prize and nothing else. This will enable you to take those chances that you are unsure of, thereby allowing you to expand your horizons and achieve levels of success that others only ever dream of.

Become the Change You Desire

The final element needed to create a success mindset is that of becoming the change you desire. One of the biggest differences between an average person and a successful person is how they perceive change. An average person will believe that the only way they will ever be happy is when the world around them changes. Alternatively, a successful person knows that in order to achieve true happiness and success, they must change their lives, becoming the change they desire. This approach puts happiness within reach by putting you in control of the decisions needed in order to create that happiness.

The first step to creating the change you desire is to visualize what that change looks like. Rather than seeing yourself as you are now, begin to imagine yourself as you want to be. Do you want to be more aggressive and bolder when it comes to making decisions? Do you want to be more at ease when meeting people for the first time? Do you want to be more confident in all areas of your life? In order to achieve these goals, you need to envision what those things look like. See yourself being bolder, more confident, more at ease. What does that look like? Does it change the way you walk, the way you dress, the way you speak? Only when you know what your best self looks like can you begin to make the changes that will transform you from who you are to who you want to be. Therefore, take the time to imagine what your ideal self looks like and write down the qualities of that self. That is the blueprint you will follow to create the life of your dreams.

The next step is to work every single day to develop your ideal self. The bigger the transformation, the more time it will take to achieve. However, each and every day can be an opportunity to focus on one quality and develop it to the max. If you want to appear more confident, focus on your posture, your stride, and how you dress on a day-to-day basis. Constantly look for ways you can improve the things that not only give the appearance of confidence, but which also engender true confidence in your heart and mind. If being more comfortable around people is your goal, then use each and every day to improve your interpersonal skills. Start by simply making eye contact with strangers or those who you want to impress; once you master that then move on to making polite conversation with those same people. By setting small goals on a daily basis, you can achieve transformation gradually, making it more natural and sustainable as a result. The key is to use the opportunities you have to become your ideal self.

The final step to creating the change you desire is to own your shortcomings. Any transformation will take time, and with each success you will face setbacks along the way. Rather than ignoring those setbacks, take the time to own them. Recognize how and why you went wrong. For example, if you fail to make eye contact with the cashier at the coffee shop, embrace the failure. Accept that you failed to take the opportunity to be your best self at that moment. Then ask yourself why it happened. If it was fear, then begin to use the techniques that turn fear into inspiration. Focus on the results of winning as opposed to the results of simply remaining as you are. By embracing your setbacks, you can turn them into learning opportunities, which will give you an even better chance of success the next time around. In the end, a success mindset is all about the direction you are traveling in. Whenever you experience successful results, you know you are on track to achieving your dreams.

Whenever you experience setbacks, you know you are off course, and thus not on track to achieving your dreams. Rather than seeing this as a failure, simply see it as an indication that you need to change course, in order to get back to chasing your dreams and thus the happy and successful life you deserve.

Chapter 11: Daily Habits for Motivation and Self-Discipline

When it comes to achieving transformation in your life, there is no magic wand that you can wave to eliminate the bad and bring in the good. Any true change requires vast amounts of time and effort to achieve. This doesn't mean that it has to be difficult, however. In fact, transformation can be relatively easy when approached from the right perspective. The trick is to break down the larger goal into smaller, more manageable goals, just as you would with any large project that you want to accomplish. One of the most effective ways to do this is to create habits that you perform on a daily basis. When you practice behavior that builds motivation and self-discipline each and every day, you will begin to transform your life one day at a time, with each result building on the last. In the course of thirty, sixty, or ninety days, the changes in the way you think and act will be nothing short of remarkable. This chapter will explore eight habits that will help create the motivation and self-discipline you need to overcome procrastination once and for all, thus enabling you to live the productive, meaningful life you are capable of.

Wake Up at a Decent Hour

The first and perhaps most important of all daily habits to form is that of waking up at a decent hour. One of the biggest mistakes most people make is that they sleep in until the very last minute, before jumping out of bed and rushing around getting ready for the day ahead. This starts the morning in a state of stress and panic, creating a negative mindset that will define the rest of the day. In order to avoid this stress and panic, it is vital that you wake up at a decent hour every day.

In addition to giving you more time to get ready, waking up at an early hour will also give you the chance to spend some quality time doing what you want to do. You might choose to go for a run, read the newspaper, catch up on social media, or simply savor a cup of your favorite coffee beverage. This act of spending time for yourself will put you in a better frame of mind all day, making you feel more important and more in control. The lack of stress and chaos will help increase your motivation for the day ahead, and the act of getting up at a set time will instill a sense of self-discipline, which will help you to take charge of all your decisions and actions for the rest of the day.

This habit needs to be performed every single day, including your days off. A bad habit that many people fall into is that of sleeping in on their days off. All this does is make it harder to wake up earlier on ordinary days. The bottom line is that your body is programmable. Therefore, it works best when it has a set, consistent routine. Changing your morning routine from one day to the next only confuses your body, adding stress to both your body and mind. Thus, practice your morning routine every single day in order to get the best results.

Perform a Small Task First Thing in the Morning

When you wake up at a decent time, it is important that you don't simply waste that extra time. Instead, it is vital that you use it to perform tasks that will help build motivation and self-discipline, and thus help you to stay in control all throughout the day. One such task might be to make your bed when you get up. Numerous studies have shown that when you make your bed first thing in the morning, it goes a long way to creating a positive mindset that will keep you motivated all day long. The reason for this is that the act of making your bed is something that benefits you and you alone. Performing a task for your benefit first thing in the morning has the effect of making you the most important person in your mind. Rather than serving your job or some other entity, it serves your wellbeing. This will help you to stay motivated as you have a higher sense of self-esteem and self-worth.

Another benefit of performing a task, such as making your bed first thing, is that it establishes self-discipline. Instead of sitting in front of the TV or turning on social media, you choose to perform a chore. This puts things into proper perspective, allowing you to keep your priorities in order. Additionally, the act of making your bed serves to keep your environment clean and organized. This will impact your state of mind, helping you to be organized in both thoughts and actions all throughout the day. Furthermore, at the end of the day when you come home, you will find your space more inviting, as it is neat and clean. This will help you to unwind more, thereby getting better rest and feeling more restored the next morning.

Visualize Your Dream

After you have performed your early morning task, the next thing you should do each day is visualize your dream. This doesn't mean contemplating all of the things you need to do in order to achieve your dream. Rather, this is the act of visualizing the big picture, the image of where you want to be, the success you crave, and the rewards you will enjoy once you turn your dream into reality. In other words, this is about visualizing the destination, not the journey.

The best way to visualize your dream is to use a visual tool, such as a vision board. As already discussed, a vision board can be covered with photos and other objects that help you to picture living the life of your dreams. Vision boards are one of the most effective tools for this purpose, but you can use any photo or item to achieve the same result. The important thing is that you spend a few quality minutes each morning focusing on your dream, so that you increase your motivation for the day ahead.

Another critical benefit that comes from visualizing your dream is that it can go a long way to keeping you in a positive mindset, no matter how your day unfolds. This is particularly true in the event that you hate your job. By focusing on your dream in the morning, you remind yourself that your present difficulties are temporary and that they may actually be serving a necessary function, one that helps you to move closer to your goals. This will keep everything in perspective, thereby helping you to transcend any stress or difficulties that rise up during the day.

Visualize Your Day

The next habit to form in your early morning hours is to visualize your day. This is a more practical exercise, one that helps you to organize and plan the day ahead. Instead of picturing your overall dream, this exercise will simply help you to visualize how you want your day to unfold. On the one hand, you can choose to visualize yourself being productive, accomplishing everything you need to that day. You can use this time to create a mental schedule of sorts, one that helps you to stay on track with your efforts all day long. This helps to increase your self-discipline by instilling a sense of purpose and direction, rather than letting you simply get caught up in the momentum of the day.

On the other hand, you might choose to visualize your day in terms of the energy you want to maintain as your day unfolds. In other words, you might visualize yourself being calm and collected in spite of any chaos surrounding you. Or you might visualize yourself as you interact with others, imagining yourself as being confident, engaging, and capable of getting your point across to everyone you talk to. The more you rehearse your day mentally, the more likely you are to put on your best performance, thus ensuring you have a good day every day.

Write Down a Task List

Visualizing your day can help to remind you of the things you want to accomplish on any given day. This leads to the next habit: writing down a task list in the morning. A task list doesn't have to be extensive—consisting of a dozen or more items that will ensure you don't get a moment to breathe before the day is done. Instead, it can consist of as few as three or four items that simply need to be accomplished within a given timeframe. The point of this exercise is twofold. First, it helps you to never forget the things you need to do by writing them down and referring to your list throughout the day. This helps to raise your productivity as well as reduce the stress caused by forgetting important tasks or errands.

Secondly, it helps you to increase your ability to recognize and remember the tasks that need to be done. By creating a list, you become more disciplined in your mindset, focusing on the important issues rather than simply allowing your thoughts to wander in any direction at all. In a way, creating a task list helps you to keep your mind focused and sharp, thereby giving you the mental self-discipline that most people lack. Your list will also make your day purpose-driven, which will help to keep you motivated and on track when others lose their drive and simply drift along.

Cross off Each Item as You Accomplish It

Once you have created your list, the next step is to begin accomplishing the tasks on it. The thing most people forget and the next habit you need to form is to cross off each item as you accomplish it. There are three main reasons why this is vital for increasing both self-discipline and motivation. First, by crossing off the items on your list, you give your list importance. If you only look at your list a couple of times a day, it will become harder and harder to keep writing it each day. It's like if you write grocery lists but always forget to take them with you when you go shopping. Eventually, you would stop making those lists since the effort would seem wasted. However, when you use your list, then the effort is validated, and it keeps you motivated to keep writing them.

The second reason why you should cross off items as you accomplish them is to help you to maintain a sense of control over your day. Rather than bouncing around from one thing to another, you have a clear direction to follow. Each time you check off an item, you remind yourself of that direction, as well as the fact that you are staying on course to achieving your goals.

Finally, there is the element of motivation. As you check off one item after another, you will build a sense of achievement, and this will help to maintain your motivation at the highest level. By the end of the day, as you check off that last item on your list, you will feel as though your day was well spent. By tracking your progress, you show just how productive you are, and this builds self-confidence and self-esteem. Therefore, instead of just meandering through each day, make sure you write a list of what you want to accomplish, big or small, and cross those items off as you go to reap the rewards.

Take Time to Reflect at the End of the Day

All successful people practice the habit of taking time to reflect at the end of the day. As little as ten minutes can go a long way to transforming your life from one of mediocrity to one of confidence, purpose, and success. The trick here is to set aside a specific time in the evening when you can be alone with your thoughts. During this time, recollect the events of the day, both good and bad. In the case of the bad events, ask yourself what went wrong and why. This isn't about self-criticism or self-loathing, rather it's about learning the lessons that setbacks can teach. If you made a mistake in how you handled a situation, recognize that mistake and determine to never repeat it. You can take this time to imagine how you could have handled the situation better, and then you can take that and apply it to your visualization practice the next morning. This is how you make steady and meaningful progress, the progress that enables you to transform your life in a real and significant way.

In the case of good events, you can take this time to relive your moments of triumph and glory. After all, it is important to celebrate each and every win, no matter how large or small. By taking the time to recall the good moments, you raise your motivation levels by recognizing your achievements. This will help you to make the right choices each and every time, thus ensuring you are your best self every single day. You can even take the time to congratulate yourself on a job well done, something that will go a long way to making you feel good about yourself. The important thing is to use this time to track your progress in terms of self-improvement. Although some days will be bad, others will be wonderful. The goal is to have your wonderful days far outnumber your bad ones.

Go to Bed at a Decent Hour

The final habit that will help you to achieve the success you both desire and deserve, is to always go to bed at a decent hour. Sleep deprivation is a common condition in the Western world. One reason for this is that many people stay up late to watch TV in an attempt to unwind from a stressful day. Unfortunately, by staying up late, they wake up tired, and this leads to even more stress and fatigue the next day. Thus, staying up late creates a vicious cycle that only serves to undermine a person's overall health and wellbeing.

By going to bed at a decent hour, you ensure you will get the sleep you need to fully recharge your batteries, both physically and mentally. This will help you to get an early start in order to establish self-discipline throughout your day. Furthermore, the more rested you are, the more energy you will have, and this will increase your motivation as well as your overall performance all day long. Therefore, while unwinding may seem like a good solution, the fact is that getting the right amount of sleep each night is the best option to take good care of your body and mind.

Additionally, once you create a regular sleep routine, your body will respond, and this will ensure that the quality of sleep you get is the absolute best. As mentioned earlier, your body is programmable. Therefore, it will respond far better when you practice the discipline of going to bed and waking up at the same time every day, than if you change your sleep pattern from one day to the next. In the end, that is why habits are so effective. As you practice habits on a daily basis, you reprogram your mind and body, and this allows you to transform your life from the one you have to the one you want. The key is to replace the bad habits that have been holding you back with the good ones that will help you to fulfill your dreams.

Chapter 12: Relapse Is Not the End of the World

This book has provided all the tools and insights you need in order to develop the behaviors and habits that will enable you to eliminate procrastination and laziness from your life. Unfortunately, the chances are you will experience setbacks along the way, specifically in terms of relapses into your old way of thinking and acting. The important thing here is to realize two vital things. First, this isn't a pass or fail scenario; therefore, it is critical that you eliminate the "all or nothing" mindset when it comes to transforming your life. Even the strongest and most determined people experience relapses; therefore, you are not alone, nor are you a failure because of it. The second thing to realize is that a relapse isn't the end of the world. Just because you have a bad day or fall back into lazy habits doesn't mean that the journey is over. A good way to think of it is like getting a flat tire on a road trip. If you get a flat tire, it doesn't mean you have to cancel your road trip and return home. All it means is that you need to fix your tire and get back on the road as soon as possible. This chapter will reveal some of the ways you can get back on the road when you experience a relapse into procrastination or laziness. By practicing these methods, you can ensure that you overcome each and every setback, continuing your journey to creating the life of your dreams.

Embrace the Setbacks

The first trick if you experience a relapse is to embrace the setback. All too often, people jump to a negative mindset in the face of a relapse, one that is full of self-criticism and shame. In the end, such a mindset only makes matters worse, often undermining self-confidence and motivation. Therefore, the best approach to any setback or relapse is to embrace it as a learning experience. See what you can learn from it and how you can grow stronger as a result.

One lesson that relapses often teach us is the value of self-care. Sometimes what causes the relapse is exhaustion or mental fatigue. This usually happens when you become too productive in your attempt to overcome procrastination and laziness. Such relapses can be a sign that your mind needs a break. In a way, it's the same situation as when your body becomes sick due to being overworked and not having enough rest. Therefore, it may be that you need to give yourself a break and take a few days off to rest and restore your energies. The chances are that after a few days you will be ready and eager to get back to your usual routine, thus proving that the setback was actually a positive experience and nothing to feel guilty about.

Another cause of a relapse is the simple lack of motivation. This can happen when you feel stuck in a rut, where your efforts aren't producing results that inspire happiness or satisfaction. In this case, the trick is to change up your routine, adding something completely new and different. Starting a new exercise regimen could jump-start your motivation, or maybe picking up a new hobby or interest will help. In the end, your relapse might just be a sign that you are tired of doing the same old thing day in and day out. Introducing a new experience or direction might be the key to getting you out of that rut and back on track to personal transformation.

In the event that a relapse is long-lasting or that you experience numerous relapses back to back, it might be an indication that the approach you are taking is not necessarily the best one for you. Taking some time to come up with a different plan is a good way to make use of a relapse, turning it into an opportunity to improve your situation overall. By coming up with a new plan, you can shift the responsibility for the relapse from you to the tools you are using. This will remove the guilt and shame that relapses can cause. Additionally, it will help to inspire you to move forward once again. Simply trying the same method over and over again will undermine your motivation if that method keeps failing. However, when you change the method, you give yourself a fresh hope, one that will give you the confidence you need to get back into the proverbial race.

Learn to Celebrate the Positives

The second trick to overcoming relapses is to celebrate the positives. One of the things about the process of self-transformation is that it is continual. You never actually reach a point where you feel as though you have made all the changes you want to make. The fact is that with each change, you discover new possibilities, and those possibilities become your next set of goals. From time to time, the constant, never-ending effort may catch up with you, causing you to feel as though you are getting nowhere. That is why taking the time to celebrate the positives can go a long way in helping you to overcome your setbacks.

One way to do this is to refer to your journal. As mentioned in this book, it is vital that you keep a journal to not only list out your goals but to also track your progress. By sitting down and reviewing your journal, you can see all of the goals you have accomplished and all the changes you have made in your life. This will show you how much progress you have made and how much your efforts have paid off. In a way, it comes down to the fact that every race has two lines, a starting line, and a finish line. When you get fixated on the fact that you haven't reached the finish line, you can become distressed and uninspired. However, if you take a moment to see how far you have come from the starting line, suddenly you see things from a different perspective. Sure, you might not be done with the race yet, but you have come a long way since you started, and that's really all that matters in the end.

Keeping track of your relapses is another way to actually stay on top of them. The simple truth is that relapses will happen, and they will happen more than once. It's a lot like accidents in the workplace. No matter how careful and conscientious people are, there will always be accidents from time to time. The trick is to make those accidents as few and far between as possible. Keeping a count of the number of days between accidents is a common practice in the workplace, showing employees how effective their efforts have been. It also serves as a motivator to keep them at their best so that the number can grow larger and larger. Counting the days between relapses can have the same effect on your motivation and sense of accomplishment. The fact is that the stronger you become, the less frequent your relapses will be. When you see the number of days growing larger between each setback, you can take pride in the progress you have made, despite the setback itself. This is how you turn a failure into a success and it's one of the most effective ways to maintain motivation, even in the hardest of times.

Seek Out Fresh Motivation

The final trick to overcoming relapses is to recharge your motivation batteries. Sometimes the things that motivated you at first become stale, resulting in them having less of an impact when it comes to inspiring you to be your best. This isn't a failure of yours, nor is it a sign that you can't accomplish your goal. Instead, it simply means that it's time for you to seek out fresh motivation. By replacing the old, worn-out quotes and memes with a fresh batch, you can rediscover the spark that enables you to forge ahead along the path of self-transformation.

One option is to watch something that motivates you. This can be anything from motivational speeches and seminars to movies that inspire you. The important thing is to find what works best for you and use that approach. If a Tony Robbins video is what gets your blood pumping, then watch one or more of them. However, if watching a movie where the main character overcomes all the odds and achieves the impossible is where you find your inner strength, then watch a few of those. Take the time to really feed your mind with fresh motivation before getting back into your day-to-day routine. This is another way of embracing the setback and using it to your advantage.

Sometimes all you need to overcome a setback is a good, strong dose of encouragement. This is why it is vital to create a support group in your life, one comprised of friends or family who can provide encouragement, advice, or just a good, strong dose of positive energy to help you get out of your rut. Taking a little time off to spend with your support group can go a long way to recharging your batteries and giving you the boost you need to jumpstart your transformation once again. In fact, your support group might be able to offer insights as to why you are struggling in the first place. One of the best things about an effective support group is that it prevents you from ever feeling as though you are all alone. Rather than having to achieve your transformation single-handedly, you can rely on the help, advice, and support of others to push past the obstacles and reach your ultimate destination—creating the life of your dreams.

Conclusion

Now that you have read *Procrastination: Discover How to Cure Laziness, Overcome Bad Habits, Develop Motivation, Improve Self-Discipline, Adopt a Success Mindset, and Increase Productivity, Even If You Are a Lazy Person*, you have all the insights and tools you need to begin eliminating procrastination from your life in every way possible. From addressing the emotional and psychological causes that keep you from pursuing your goals to overcoming the bad habits that undermine your productivity, you will be able to start accomplishing any task or project you set your mind to. Additionally, by introducing good habits into your day-to-day life, you can begin to transform your life, using each and every day to create the life of your dreams. Finally, when you begin to replace lazy habits and tendencies with productive, purpose-driven habits and tendencies, you will begin to develop higher levels of self-confidence and self-esteem, thereby improving your life in every way imaginable. In short, by practicing the methods and techniques in this book, you will discover and fulfill your true potential, thus becoming your ideal self. Good luck on your journey to achieving the success you both desire and deserve!

Sources

https://www.youtube.com/watch?v=7DvftaHlZR0

https://www.developgoodhabits.com/causes-of-procrastination/

https://www.psychologicalscience.org/observer/why-wait-the-science-behind-procrastination

https://www.youtube.com/watch?v=TY3k4KbpuUg

https://medium.com/swlh/how-procrastination-is-a-direct-consequence-of-low-self-esteem-31005971ce1e

https://www.psychologytoday.com/intl/blog/fulfillment-any-age/201204/the-paradox-procrastination

https://www.youtube.com/watch?v=gd7wAithl7I

https://academichelp.net/uncategorized/differences-procrastination-and-laziness.html

https://incredibleplanet.net/the-difference-between-laziness-and-procrastination/

https://www.youtube.com/watch?v=9_gu7e5L-wg

http://yourpositivitycoach.com/why-negative-thoughts-create-discouragement-and-lack-of-motivation/

https://www.youtube.com/watch?v=dopb3jBlrXc

https://www.psychologytoday.com/us/blog/dont-delay/201803/how-negative-thoughts-relate-procrastination

https://www.developgoodhabits.com/mental-models/

https://www.youtube.com/watch?v=wmx_35rQIRg

https://www.youtube.com/watch?v=adDgQeRavzU

https://www.youtube.com/watch?v=OQLdyPuF6ig

https://gettingthingsdone.com/2017/04/10-tips-for-success-with-gtd/

https://dev.to/duomly/10-tips-to-increase-your-productivity-and-get-things-done-3n3e

https://thezeroed.com/steps-effective-goal-setting/

https://www.makeuseof.com/tag/start-project-now-dont-feel-like/

https://www.youtube.com/watch?v=3-embFrOVL4

https://www.developgoodhabits.com/bad-productivity-habits/

https://www.acquirent.com/what-is-a-success-mindset/

https://www.youtube.com/watch?v=1vIvnNEyB-w

https://www.youtube.com/watch?v=MmfikLimeQ8

https://www.youtube.com/watch?v=-71zdXCMU6A

https://gregandfionascott.com/success-mindset-2/

https://thriveglobal.com/stories/5-steps-to-develop-a-success-mindset/

https://www.lifeoptimizer.org/2017/04/06/motivation-vs-self-discipline-habit-formation/

https://medium.com/personal-growth-lab/6-daily-habits-to-make-motivation-flow-effortlessly-c4156661e221

https://vocal.media/motivation/10-methods-to-improve-self-discipline

https://www.positivityblog.com/how-to-stop-being-so-lazy/

https://stephaniepollock.com/5-helpful-project-steps/

https://www.livescience.com/20026-brain-dopamine-worker-slacker.html

https://www.nytimes.com/1986/12/02/science/major-personality-study-finds-that-traits-are-mostly-inherited.html

Here's another book by Deon Hilman that you might be interested in

LAZINESS

What You Need to Know to Cure Procrastination, Master Time Management and Develop Self-discipline Like a Spartan of Incredible Mental Toughness

DEON HILLMAN

Printed in Great Britain
by Amazon